Conversations to Change Teaching

CRITICAL PRACTICE IN HIGHER EDUCATION

Acknowledgements

We would like to thank colleagues and students who have worked with us, and have had conversations with us, over many years and who have helped to develop our thinking and practice. We thank the anonymous book proposal reviewers, particularly the one who commented that there was no point in writing this book, as no one has time for conversations in universities anymore. This helped us to focus on being both aspirational and realistic. Thank you to colleagues who read drafts of the text: Claire Dickerson, Angela Hammond, Karen Smith and Amanda Roberts. Finally we acknowledge our debt to Sally Graham who was an inspirational colleague. The influence of her 'conversations to change teaching' continues in the lives of so many.

Conversations to Change Teaching

Joy Jarvis and Karen Clark

Series Editors: Joy Jarvis and Karen Smith

CRITICAL PRACTICE IN HIGHER EDUCATION

First published in 2020 by Critical Publishing Ltd

The authors have made every effort to ensure the accuracy of information contained in this publication, but assume no responsibility for any errors, inaccuracies, inconsistencies and omissions. Likewise, every effort has been made to contact copyright holders. If any copyright material has been reproduced unwittingly and without permission the Publisher will gladly receive information enabling them to rectify any error or omission in subsequent editions.

British Library Cataloguing in Publication Data
A CIP record for this book is available from the British Library

ISBN: 9781913063771

This book is also available in the following e-book formats:
MOBI ISBN: 9781913063788
EPUB ISBN: 9781913063795
Adobe e-book ISBN: 9781913063801

Cover design by Out of House Limited
Text design by Greensplash Limited
Project Management by Newgen Publishing UK
Printed and bound in the UK by 4edge, Essex

Critical Publishing
3 Connaught Road
St Albans
AL3 5RX

www.criticalpublishing.com

Paper from responsible sources

Contents

Meet the **authors and series editors**

Karen Clark is Programme Leader of a Postgraduate Certificate in Learning and Teaching in Higher Education at the University of Hertfordshire, which attracts colleagues from every academic school at the institution. She is engaged with a range of work involving professional learning and recognition, curriculum development and staff–student collaboration. She draws on conversations about teaching both formal and informal in many different contexts from peer review, programme development and teaching observation to lunch groups and chats fuelled by coffee and cake.

Joy Jarvis is currently Professor of Educational Practice at the University of Hertfordshire and a UK National Teaching Fellow. She has experience in a wide range of education contexts and works to create effective learning experiences for students and colleagues. She is particularly interested in the professional learning of those engaged in educational practice in higher education settings and has undertaken a range of projects, working with colleagues locally, nationally and internationally, to develop practice in teaching and leadership of teaching. Joy works with doctoral students exploring aspects of educational practice and encourages them to be adventurous in their methodological approaches and to share their findings in a range of contexts to enable practice change.

Karen Smith is Reader in Higher Education in the School of Education at the University of Hertfordshire. She has a strong research interest in transnational education, notably in flying faculty models and is author of the *Transnational Education Toolkit* for the Higher Education Academy. Karen spent many years working on lecturer development programmes and is now the Director of the University of Hertfordshire's Professional Doctorate in Education. Karen also leads collaborative research and development in her School, where she engages in externally funded research and evaluation and supports the development of scholarly educational practice through practitioner research.

Book summary

We believe that conversations have the power to change teaching in higher education at individual, group and institutional levels. We have written this book to share our ideas, drawn from our own practice and building on the work of others, to show how this might be achieved. We argue that conversation undertaken purposefully is a professional learning tool that can be available to all. We appreciate that the current context may not be conducive to conversation, so we aim to show how it can be built into everyday work practices. We hope that academics new to teaching, their more experienced colleagues and institutional leaders of teaching will find the ideas for practice useful and that the book can be a focus for conversation that will lead to change.

Why this book?

The authors of this book work to facilitate the development of staff learning about teaching in a university. Joy comes from an education background, is a National Teaching Fellow and in her role as Professor of Educational Practice works in a range of informal ways with staff from different disciplines to share ideas and approaches to teaching. Karen has a background in teaching law and is a member of a central team which offers a number of opportunities for professional learning for academic staff across the university, including a postgraduate programme, a professional recognition scheme and a variety of workshops. We have worked together during the past ten years to structure opportunities for conversation between academic staff members with the purpose of changing practice. We have learned a great deal about the processes and the challenges involved.

We decided to write this book together because we believe that talk about university teaching has the potential to change the lives of students, staff and institutions and that currently it is undervalued and underused. Metrics, target-setting and performance measures mean the focus of conversation can struggle to get beyond procedures and organisation. Increasingly complex academic roles, work pressures and job insecurity encourage the idea that talking about teaching is really only for those with specific management roles for education. Academic communities working under pressure do not prioritise ways to develop and embed disciplinary learning practices together.

In this book, we aim to raise the profile of conversation and its potential for bringing about change in the way teaching is thought about and undertaken. We will draw on our own experience and research along with examples of practice from a range of different institutions.

We argue that conversation is an essential activity for both individual and institutional well-being and effectiveness. It is a powerful, underappreciated and often unexplored tool within the reach of all. The ubiquity of talk can distract from the significance of purposeful, deliberate conversation which might be used to chip away at the very obstacles which appear to squeeze it from our professional lives.

Stimulating dialogue in both formal and informal settings can combat the isolation which often characterises university teaching practice, can enable us to reach effective collegiate responses to complex and evolving challenges, and has the potential to restore value to some of those processes which can all too easily slide into hollow bureaucracy.

Talking about our teaching enables us to articulate what we value and how that plays out in the lecture hall, seminar room, laboratory or studio. We argue that valuable conversation with colleagues can still be achieved in our congested working lives and that developing the skills to make the most of every opportunity can make an important contribution to the robustness of university teaching in an increasingly demanding environment. The key question we ask in this book is 'how can we use conversation to change teaching?'

Why conversation?

Conversation happens so frequently that we hardly notice it. However, it can have powerful and long-lasting effects. In this book, we explore ways of having conversations about teaching that can influence us, our colleagues and institutions. For this to happen we need space, though not always much, as brief corridor conversations can have a big impact (Haig, 2006). Indeed, most of us can probably recall conferences and meetings when we felt that the most learning happened in moments of chat over coffee, outside the formal structure of the sessions. A feature of the type of conversations we are proposing is a level of informality that flattens power relations and enables people to make meaning together. It is about people trying to make sense of an issue, drawing from their experience and knowledge of the field. It involves listening to the ideas of others, trying to articulate our own thoughts and building towards some form of agreement on the topic – even if that is to agree to differ.

When our diaries are packed, informal routine conversations with teaching peers seem to be a luxury: 'there's no time for coffee these days'. However, we argue that it is vital to protect such interactions. Anecdotes and stories about classroom events that are often told on these occasions can build greater understanding of participants' practice and the thinking that underpins it. In fact, we would argue that this shared professional learning also makes us more efficient when it comes to deliberation in more formal contexts such as planning meetings and programme review. Far from being a waste of time, it ensures we make the best of it.

The term 'conversation' has been used in a range of ways by writers exploring its use. Senge (1990, p 9), for example, talks about 'learningful' conversations *'that balance inquiry and advocacy, where people expose their own thinking effectively and make that thinking open to the influence of others'*. This approach involves the use of dialogue, again a concept used in different ways, but here we draw particularly on the ideas of Bohm (1996). He distinguishes dialogue from discussion, in which people identify and analyse their own views and try to 'win the game'. Discussion can then move on to negotiation, where individual positions are held less strongly and this can be a preliminary stage in dialogue. Dialogue itself involves *'opening up judgements and assumptions'* (Bohm, 1996, p 46) so that something new can form in the space in between. At this stage participants can stand back from their own assumptions, identify them, recognise the personal and cultural influences that informed them and then create something new in relation to the topic. Teaching approaches, curricula and a whole range of practice developments can then be created, for as Zeldin notes (1998, p 14), *'when minds meet they don't just exchange facts; they transform them, draw implications from them, engage in new trains of thought. Conversation doesn't just reshuffle the cards; it creates new cards.'* These 'new cards' could include an idea for a session, a change in assessment strategy or a completely new way of seeing practice. Conversations like this involve people thinking together, or 'interthinking' (Littleton and Mercer, 2013, p 26), with the potential of creating *'a new kind of understanding that neither could have achieved alone'*.

Conversation can help evolve individual practice, it can contribute to professional ways of working within disciplinary teams and it can fuel reflection and stimulate change around accepted assumptions across an institution. We argue that its goal should be this disruption of individual, group and institutional ways of thinking and acting. Here the term disruption is used *'in the sense of adopting a stance of questioning, challenging and critiquing taken-for-granted ways of doing things in higher education'* (Quinn, 2012, p 1). Such disturbance could be seen as a problem where there is a very hierarchical management of teaching. We explore this and other challenges of leading change through a conversational approach throughout the book and particularly in the final chapter.

Conversation requires attention as well as talking, and we will consider examples of listening and questioning strategies to enable effective dialogue. Any exchange can be derailed or limited by power, status or unexplored and conflicting conceptions of how teaching quality might be identified; we explore different approaches to reduce the impact of these factors.

We look at different ways to equip ourselves for conversations that can prompt change. We argue that participants must be prepared in terms of personal communication skills, subject knowledge and an understanding of different contexts. We must also be able to identify and willing to seize conversational opportunities, including those that happen as part of normal practice, such as peer review, staff induction, professional recognition procedures or the daily organisation of teaching. We explore ways we have worked in groups to sustain conversations over time and raise questions about what it means to lead through this type of dialogue. Above all, we aim to identify why it is important to talk about teaching and what can happen if we do.

Why talk about teaching?

Conversation about teaching in higher education sometimes does not get beyond discussion of organisation, timetables and procedures, all of which are important but are part of the systems around teaching rather than the core of practice. At the centre of teaching is the purpose and process of student learning, and it is talk about this with which we are concerned. Disciplinary knowledge, professional standards, technology, procedures and views of education continually change the setting in which we teach, so we must be both proactive and responsive. This requires us to take an 'inquiry stance' (Cochran-Smith and Lytle, 2009), exploring our professional and personal knowledge, practices and values. We must both keep up-to-date in relation to our discipline or profession and pay attention to what is happening in the classroom and to learners' development. But more than this, we need to adopt a disposition to question our teaching. Conversations can help – sharing relevant research findings and other evidence and considering how it fits within our own practice.

We take it as given that teaching is neither straightforward nor common sense, two descriptions sometimes given to the process. As Cochran-Smith (2004, p 298) identifies, teaching is *'an intellectual, cultural, and contextual activity that requires skilful decisions about how to convey subject matter knowledge, apply pedagogical skills, develop human relationships and both generate and utilize local knowledge'.*

As disciplinary experts or professional teachers we will have understandings, assumptions, values and ways of acting that have become part of who we are in the classroom. Much of this may be held tacitly (Eraut, 2000) and conversations within and beyond our discipline can help to 'unpack' what we know, which in turn can enable us to make these things explicit to students (Schön, 1987). Conversations with those outside our field are particularly useful at illuminating differing assumptions. However, dialogue with our disciplinary peers is essential to elicit the ways of teaching and learning in a particular field. This is known as 'pedagogical content knowledge' (Shulman, 2004) and is central to disciplinary teaching. As Kreber (2009, p 28) notes: *'Reflection on pedagogical content knowledge encourages faculty to explore why, within their own departments, teaching is approached in a particular way'.*

In this text we also consider how talking with students about their learning, as opposed to merely gathering data from satisfaction surveys, is invaluable. It can enable insight into different perspectives, a greater shared understanding of why teaching is undertaken in particular ways and can explore enhancement of practice. Teaching is designed to facilitate learning but cannot, of course, ensure that this happens. Conversations about learning and teaching between staff and students can enable greater clarity of purpose and, as we illustrate through examples, can be undertaken in a range of ways.

In a paper produced for the UK Higher Education Academy (Stevenson et al, 2014) the authors argue for more dialogue and critical reflection on teaching at all levels across institutions so that it does not become driven by external agendas that may not align with the values and principles of staff and students. A concept of 'pedagogical frailty', developed in relation to the systems that support teaching, suggests that if values and practices are not aligned this can lead to inauthentic practice and lack of personal investment in developing and changing teaching (Kinchin and Winstone, 2017; Jarvis, 2018). Conversations can help to connect values and practice. Creating opportunities for reflective inquiry conversations among practitioners can pull together the expertise of all involved and enable an orientation to inquiry as an ongoing approach to organisational change and development.

Changing teaching through conversations

There is increasing interest in conversation as part of change and development practice in higher education. Coaching, for example, '*a method of work-related learning which relies primarily on one-to-one-conversations*' (de Haan and Burger, 2014, p 5) is used in a number of universities (eg Graham and Weston, 2013) to engage colleagues in learning from and with each other. The idea of 'mentoring communities' (Felten et al, 2013, p 20) where higher education colleagues use '*sustained conversation to assist one another*' connects with the notion that work colleagues learn together in '*communities of practice*' (Wenger et al, 2002). While legitimate reservations have been raised about the way this concept has been used, its central idea that colleagues have the expertise to learn together for the benefit of themselves and their institutions underpins the processes we explore.

Of course, some university staff do have conversations with one another about teaching and do appreciate their value. Roxa and Martensson (2009) in a study of 109 academics found that those staff who talked about teaching did so with a small number of chosen colleagues in private, informal conversations which bore no direct relation to organisational or departmental units. They found that these 'significant networks' were where individuals tested ideas about teaching and devised ways to solve their teaching challenges. In this book, we explore how such conversations about teaching can be enhanced by scholarship, including reading about and researching practice, and by support and challenge from colleagues in a range of settings. We would like to encourage colleagues to purposefully prepare, plan and engage in the practice of talking about teaching.

This might begin with asking questions such as:

» What is good/less good about current ways of doing things?

» Are these approaches aligned with our values and purposes?

» What issues are raised and by whom?

» Why are these issues being raised?

» What have others done in similar contexts?

» What could we try? Why?

» How would we know if it is working?

Such questions could be raised at the level of classroom practice, in relation to a disciplinary-based programme or to teaching in the whole institution. They could narrow to focus on individual practice or encourage the addressing of issues of ideology and values and how they are realised in university practice. All types of questions can be explored through conversations, if people in different roles are prepared to take the risk to do this. It is a risk because the potential for disruption is inherent in the process of conversation and while this can produce creative action it will involve challenge. The idea of an individual taking an inquiry stance to their practice may be seen as fairly straightforward, but an approach to organisational change that encourages groups to inquire into practice through conversational approaches, rather than structured meetings about implementing strategy, can be difficult to envisage and of necessity unpredictable and therefore difficult to control. Nevertheless, in a complex changing environment where practice is created in social contexts all participants will influence that practice to some extent (Stacey, 2001). Much of the work on conversation and change at organisational level relates to ideas of complexity and the role of communication and sense-making which sees change as a *participative practice* (Shaw, 2002, p 21). Colleagues using this approach argue that change happens in relationships between people in an organisation and develops through 'conversational activity' (Flinn and Mowles, 2014). This highlights the significance of conversations in all parts of the organisation for effecting change and also the importance for leadership of teaching of paying attention to the conversations in which we are all involved.

The aim of taking a conversational approach is to build a process of ongoing change and development rather than being stuck in 'presentism' (Hargreaves, 2008) which inhibits lasting improvement. In a context of presentism the institution becomes 'addicted' to devising solutions in response to a particular issue and not addressing medium or longer-term practice development across the whole context. Higher education institutions must deal with many external drivers in relation to league tables, which without care can lead to a piecemeal approach to change that fails to build staff capacity and agency to lead their own practice development.

This book is designed both for colleagues with all levels of experience who are leading their own learning in teaching, and for those who aim to lead the professional learning of others. We use the terms 'lecturer' and 'teacher' interchangeably; one term being the job title of many colleagues engaged in teaching while the other identifies more fully the role of the educator. Throughout the text we give examples of our own practice, because showing what we have done and critiquing it can enable colleagues to begin to answer the question 'what shall we do in practice?' We also look at others' practice, ask questions to provoke thinking and identify some texts that can help to build learning conversations.

Critical questions for practice

» Do you make time to talk about your teaching with trusted colleagues?

» Do you approach challenges about teaching with a willingness to inquire into and change your practice?

» Do you think you respond to immediate external pressures at the expense of considered long-term thinking about teaching?

Summary

• Current processes and pressures frequently squeeze out essential dialogue about teaching.

• Purposeful conversation should be at the heart of effective academic development.

• Attention must be given to practice in order to develop deep understanding of disciplinary ways of teaching.

• Conversation can enable all to contribute to successful evolution of their institutions.

Useful texts

Baker, A, Jensen, P and Kolb, D (2002) *Conversational Learning: An Experiential Approach to Knowledge Creation.* Westport, CT: Quorum Books.

This edited text explores different aspects of learning through conversation and would be useful for readers interested in looking at the theoretical underpinnings of learning through conversations.

Haig, N (2006) Everyday Conversation as a Context for Professional Learning and Development. *International Journal for Academic Development,* 10(1): 3–16.

In this accessible article a learning and teaching developer reflects on his own use of conversation as a development tool and how and why it works.

A chance for talk within everyone's reach

We begin our consideration of how conversations can be used to change teaching with institutionally organised peer review: usually an annual pairing of academics involving observation of practice or review of resources. It is for many one of the few formal moments in the yearly cycle when they are expected to talk about teaching. It offers an opportunity for valuable dialogue and yet a great number of us will have experienced it at least on occasion as an empty and possibly stressful exercise. In this chapter, we suggest an approach which might enable us to embrace the process and derive value from it.

We decided to look first at these conversations because peer review is used in most higher education institutions in the UK and many other countries, although the extent to which it is useful is unclear (Klopper and Drew, 2015). Once a session or online learning materials have been observed there is usually a conversation and some form of paperwork to complete as evidence of participation in the process. The sessions or learning materials can involve teaching face to face or online. The exchange may involve colleagues from a single institution or include national or international partners.

Although we are clearly free to consider these encounters in whatever way we choose, their mandating by institutions and 'reporting back' mechanisms can make them feel like supervision or monitoring. Despite the process involving peers and not assessors, there is a *'tendency to associate the observation of teaching with the idea that a peer is judging the quality of the teaching observed'* (Gosling, 2014, p 15). Understanding this to be the case prompted us to explore the practice using the popular television programme *The Great British Bake Off*, in which contestants bake and judges assess the quality of their cakes and biscuits. By using a familiar format, which we describe further below, we were able to highlight with humour some frequently unquestioned assumptions with which peer review is often approached.

Conversation is an expected aspect of peer review no matter how an institution organises the procedure, though in reality this may be brief and instrumental. We look at ways to facilitate learning both as observer and observee. We draw on some key concepts, which are developed in later chapters, such as inquiry, critical reflection on teaching and noticing practice. We also offer examples from our own experience.

Preparing the ground for a professional conversation is vital to maximise learning, as power dynamics can otherwise easily derail the exchange. If colleagues are able to shape a focus on mutual learning then this can enhance their dialogue. If both approach the experience accepting *'parity of power relations'* and *'reciprocity of learning'* (Gosling 2014, p 22) they can together build an effective context for conversations about teaching.

Preparation for conversation: the observed session

Some discussion between the paired academics before the review, whether a brief conversation or email exchange, can be useful to establish a shared expectation of the purpose and process of the activity. Even where both are interested in teaching, if one is expecting judgement and the other professional discussion then the result can be a wasted opportunity, as Karen recalls.

Critical issues

Misaligned expectations

I was an enthusiastic but relatively inexperienced tutor and was pleased to learn that a colleague with a reputation as a good teacher was to observe me. I understood the exercise to be an endorsement or otherwise of my practice. The only aspect of our debrief I really heard at the time and can recall now is that she told me about a student who was not included in the group work I had organised. I felt as though I was doing badly and was discouraged. I contrast this with a review some years later with a colleague with whom I had already had many conversations about teaching. We both saw this as an opportunity to improve a difficult session I'd battled with and I embraced her extensive discussion of the challenges in the way my colleague years before had no doubt hoped I would. For me the key difference was one of expectation.

Equally, if the observee expects discussion and the observer feels obliged to deliver judgement then the exchange can be frustrating. Identifying in advance what is uppermost in each lecturer's mind with regard to their teaching can prevent them talking at cross-purposes. In review of a taught session, the observee will often have a heightened awareness of classroom events and they will notice what is particularly salient to them in the broader context of what they consider to be good teaching and their knowledge of the student group or topic. 'Noticing' is something we do to a certain extent all the time but as Mason (2002, p 9) notes, *'there is so much more we could notice'*. What we see in a session will be influenced by our own frame of reference, which derives from a range of influences including culture, professional context, discipline, experience, knowledge about teaching and our values. The same is true of the observer, who will notice what is important to them. Each frame of reference will be different; what is noticed will therefore differ and the perception of what happened in the session may contrast significantly, as illustrated by Joy's account below. These differences can in themselves enrich the discussion, while failure to appreciate them can undermine conversation as colleagues talk at cross-purposes.

Critical issues

Frames of reference and making assumptions

I was observed when working with students in a prison context. My observer commented that the students weren't sitting properly at their desks. I was confused as I hadn't noticed an issue, and in the conversation after the session I did explain that one student preferred to stand and put his work on the top of a filing cabinet as he had difficulty sitting still. The observer said that the issue was that the other students were 'slouching' and clearly 'couldn't be bothered to engage'. I hadn't noticed any slouching; I felt that the students' quality of work contrasted with this perception based on body language that they weren't engaged.

I made a similar assumption when observing students in a colleague's undergraduate session at a university. They were leaning back on their chairs and in some cases seemed asleep, but the quality of their questions and discussion following the lecture, and the conversations I had with individual students, showed them to be highly motivated and interested and that they had learned a great deal in the session.

It is very easy to make assumptions, particularly when observing a session, and to ascribe motivations to body language, interactions and events. Assumptions, as Mason (2002) notes, close down opportunities for thinking whereas we are hoping to open them up. Expressions such as 'couldn't be bothered' are inferences based on assumptions and can lead to misconceptions and lack of professional learning. So, an observer who notes, 'the students hadn't bothered to do the pre-reading for the session' could lead the conversation down the road of blaming students and effectively exclude other explanations. By contrast, if the observer keeps a simple note of what happens such as '20 of the 30 students hadn't read the pre-session text in full', assumptions are avoided and a variety of possibilities can be explored.

Because both participants will notice what is significant to them it is important that the observer has a clear idea before the session of what their colleague wishes to focus upon. Novice tutors whose view of teaching is as yet unexplored may initially battle to pinpoint this, and when asked may simply say 'everything' or identify only more presentational matters (eg 'Am I speaking too fast/loudly enough?'). In such circumstances it can be easy to slip into the trap of fixating on more generic aspects such as participation in group activities while failing to explore students' key learning of concepts and evidence of disciplinary thinking. However, if both share an understanding of the context and purpose of the session and then engage in the systematic noticing described below this should enable a productive dialogue. If the observer is able to note what happens in some detail, including student questions or answers, this supports a rich dialogue. The observee, who is the subject expert, can then explain disciplinary aspects of learning and teaching. Talking with students, if appropriate, about their learning can also be valuable to understand their thinking and perceptions.

The conversation about teaching and the review paperwork is generally completed shortly after the teaching session it relates to, as the experience is fresh and easy to recall. One way of limiting the tendency of one person to judge the other's teaching is for both observer and observee to watch each other's sessions before a paired discussion. This can enable a clearer focus on teaching approaches and the learning of both participants, although it loses the immediacy of a prompt exchange.

The paperwork

Peer review procedure normally includes paperwork that must be completed and sometimes this is drafted in a way that does not readily encourage the professional conversation for which we suggest colleagues might aim. The person whose session is being observed often records details of the topic, student group, aims and objectives of the session to set the context. The observer may be expected to comment on such criteria as 'clarity of PowerPoint slides', or 'quality of spoken language'; they may even be required to note 'perceived strengths and areas for improvement of the session'. Without care this may create a focus on aspects that may have limited importance in a particular session and can encourage the writing of judgemental statements. One way forward could be to use such official paperwork only at the end of the peer review process to complete what is required by the institution for recording purposes.

Rather than focusing on externally developed criteria during the observation it can be useful to write a narrative of the session. Noting times when something occurs can be helpful during the subsequent conversation as the person teaching may over or underestimate how long something took, and this information can inform a discussion about the pace of the session or how time was used. The observer may also want to note what they are thinking at the time so this can be returned to during the conversation or inform the observer's own teaching. Below is an example of part of a narrative of an observed session.

Example 2.1

Notes from an observed session

Time	Narrative	Thoughts
08.55	Students come into the lecture theatre, see the 'please do not sit in this row' notices at the back of the room and fill up the first six rows. About 50 students are present. About half take out notepads and pens. 15 students open laptops.	How did you explain this to the students at the beginning of the module or is this the first time you've done this? I wonder if this would help in my large lecture where people sit in small groups all round the lecture theatre?
	You walk along the front row and up the steps asking if people had a good rest after the field trip last week and talking about the rain during the final day.	I tend to stand behind the podium from the start to signal that this topic is serious and we need to get on – it would be good to discuss the advantages and disadvantages of these approaches.
09.05	You hold up various items of equipment and ask students to name them and say what they were used for on the field trip. Students call out answers and you repeat these.	I found I couldn't hear what all the students said so it was great that you repeated their words using the mike. I wondered why you brought in all the practical items when pictures on the screen could have been used.
	You then ask them to talk in pairs and then in fours about what they think was missing from the field-trip items that is essential to the work.	I wondered why you asked them to talk with each other at this point – I don't do this in my sessions in case I can't get them quiet again.

Time	Narrative	Thoughts
09.15	As far as I could tell all the students, except one, seemed to be engaging in the discussion. He was looking at his mobile.	
	You put up the first slide which has a web link and ask one person in each group of four to use their mobile phone to use this link to put up the groups' ideas on the screen.	I would like to discuss the use of mobile phones in the classroom.
	About 25 words are put up.	
	You quickly go through each of the responses – many are the same. You agree that the items, including sandwiches, are useful. Most of the students are laughing at this point.	
	You then put up a group picture of the students taken at the end of the trip – they all seem to be looking at this and laughing. You point out that *they* are the missing element we need to talk about, as they will be interpreting the data.	I would be interested to discuss why you did the intro this way – I would have put up the interpreting data slide first and then the intended learning outcomes – it would be good to discuss session introductions.
	Your next slide is 'Interpreting Data – what questions are we asking?'	

This short excerpt from observation notes already raises a host of topics for exploration. What is important for the learning of both parties is how the subsequent conversation is undertaken.

The conversation

As discussed earlier, there needs to be clarity about the purpose of the conversation held after the teaching session. In our experience this exchange can be much more fruitful if a 'Bake-off', assessor style, approach is avoided. In the TV programme

'Bake-Off' judges assess the quality of cakes baked by contestants. We argue that in peer review observers should not see themselves as judges in this way, but rather partners in a shared professional dialogue. To explore this with colleagues we developed a list of statements that contrast the role of judge with that of a critical friend (Table 2.1).

Table 2.1 Differences between judges and peer observers.

Bake-off judge	Peer observer
My role is to act as judge	My role is to act as a critical friend
My role is to evaluate	My role is to enable my colleague to think critically
I am an expert in this field	I have some professional knowledge about teaching but I am not an expert in teaching this topic in this context
I need to be explicit about what I think is good and bad	I need to enable my colleague to identify and reflect on aspects of teaching and learning
What I think is most important	How I enable my colleague to think is most important
This is a key learning opportunity for my colleague	I'm keen to learn through this process
I believe there's a correct way of doing things and I need to assess if my colleague is doing it right	I believe that through engaging in a peer inquiry we will both learn
I need to use this opportunity to improve my colleague's practice	I need to use this opportunity to improve my own practice

The reason we wrote these contrasting statements is that in practice peer observers too often resemble Bake-off judges! This is partly because peer observation can be construed as a teaching quality monitoring system and because, as noted above, the paperwork can drive observers into judgement. Also once a pattern of observation as judgement is established it is difficult to dismantle and it tends to self-perpetuate. We consider the purpose of peer review to be that both parties, and particularly the observee, will be prompted to new thinking and practice about their teaching. It is important to keep this goal in mind.

We see three principles underpinning successful peer review: inquiry, reflection and criticality. This conversation is a rare opportunity to share thinking with a colleague about teaching and to have time to go into the depth needed to explore and develop ideas. If it is to be successful then it needs to include these principles.

Principles

Inquiry

Taking an inquiry approach to one's teaching in this context means asking questions about what is happening in a particular session, why it might be happening and how one could collect evidence to extend one's understanding of the situation and how it could be developed or changed. Having an observer in a session is one way of collecting some evidence. Taking an inquiry approach focuses on the learning, and the teaching that facilitates this learning, and is not about a 'performance'. Teaching is highly contextual; a session which seems to work well with one group may turn out to be inappropriate for another. This means that one cannot use rules or prescriptions but must be attentive and responsive in the moment. Taking an 'inquiry stance' (Cochran-Smith and Lytle, 2009) to one's teaching is a powerful approach to ongoing improvement. An effective peer observation conversation will support skills and dispositions to question and explore examples of practice and engagement in this form of professional learning.

Reflection

A key element in learning as a professional is thinking about examples of practice that have taken place and drawing lessons from these. Schön (1987) looked at different professional groups and identified that 'reflection on action', thinking back over an example of practice, was important in learning from experience. Questions posed by an observer during a peer review conversation, such as 'Why did you decide to ...?' can prompt reflection. The observer may also notice an observee's actions that they were not aware of, for example: 'I noticed that when a student asked a question in the classroom, you always repeated it'. Or 'I noticed that you always checked the equipment twice before you started each experiment'. Sometimes unconscious knowledge of teaching or disciplinary practice can become explicit through this form of discussion. This knowledge can then be used for planning and for sharing with students who are getting to grips with practices in their discipline.

Criticality

All staff will encourage criticality in their students. In the same way reflection and inquiry into teaching practice needs to be critical. This can be supported by considering alternative perspectives and different sources of evidence drawn from the peer review partner's own experience, student perspectives and appropriate reading. There are many ways to collect relevant evidence from students about their learning, such as answers to a question written on a sticky note or using online discussion boards.

Examples from experience can be drawn on to support inquiry; it is more helpful to frame these as statements such as 'I found when I tried X ...' rather than being directive 'I think you should do X'. Research and writing in the field enables a wider range of evidence to be considered. Journals devoted to disciplinary teaching, as well as more general education texts, can be useful for challenging current thinking.

The conversational approach

The observer in peer review does not need to have expertise in the particular disciplinary teaching undertaken in the observed session, but does need to have skills in creating a context for a 'learning conversation' as discussed in the first chapter. The space needs to be suitable for a relaxed and focused conversation and an environment where power hierarchies are as limited as possible.

When using the 'Bake-off' theme while exploring peer review with colleagues we identified some 'ingredients' which could make the conversation effective and drew on Kline (1999) and Thomson (2013) in particular for ideas in relation to listening (Figure 2.1).

INGREDIENTS

Context

Preparing time, space, location

Creating a physical environment that says 'this is important for us'

Attentive listening

The observer listens twice as much as they talk

Paraphrasing is used to check understanding – 'you are saying that x is important'

Summarising helps to focus learning – 'we think x worked well to encourage alternative perspectives'

Questioning

Open questions – 'what did you think about X?'

Probing questions – 'why do you think the students did X?'

Observational and inquiring statements

'I noticed...'

'I'm curious to know more about...'

Figure 2.1 Ingredients for an effective peer review conversation.

While good ingredients are important for a good cake, it is the skill of the baker that determines the outcome. The process of the peer review conversation needs to be undertaken so that it leads to a positive outcome, which we see as being both parties learning and feeling positive and energised about taking actions to develop practice. An example of the beginning of a conversation about teaching is given in the example below. It draws on the observation notes presented earlier. We use O for observer and T for the person teaching the session.

Example 2.2

Conversation following an observation

O: Well I found that really interesting – I hadn't been to a session on that topic before.

T: I've taught it to about five groups so far this year but each group is different so I never know exactly how it will go.

O: How did you think this one went?

T: Better than last week when the technology failed! Although technology isn't essential to this session.

O: Later I would be interested to talk with you about technology, particularly the use of mobile phones which is one thing I noticed, but first I would be interested to know what you noticed about the session.

T: I suppose I noticed that I tend to make assumptions about what students know and how they see this field. I was a bit thrown by the suggestion from a student that they should be given the questions in advance when doing fieldwork – rather than generating their own questions. It made me think about doing some general stuff about the role of the scientist and the way we are as scientists and what we are doing in these sessions, which is not just about subject content but is about being a scientist.

O: How do you think you might do this?

T: Not sure. It will need thinking about. One thing I could do is to say why I am doing certain things rather than just doing them. I do this in the field, it's natural, but in the lecture theatre I tend to think about content and expect them to see what I'm doing. Well really I hadn't thought about this aspect before.

O: Was there anything else that stood out for you?

T: I really noticed the young man in the back at the end of the row – he wasn't talking with the other students. I also noticed that once I got to the stats slides a number of students got on their phones. I wasn't sure if they were checking terminology or texting their friends. I was conscious of time and didn't want to stop but I felt I lost a lot of people's attention about 40 minutes in.

We ran a session for staff on peer review using video examples of teaching and then we acted out conversations in the manner of the one above, where following on from this beginning the subsequent exploratory talk identified key questions and ideas about teaching for both participants. Some colleagues felt that the observer in the conversation should be more assertive. The comment 'you need to tell them what is wrong with the teaching' was typical. This shows the pervasiveness of a 'Bake-off' approach. Clearly challenge is important for any development or change and all of us need to see what could be improved in order to have the motivation to change. However, feeling defensive about our teaching due to someone judging our work on a snapshot of practice is unlikely to lead to change. We explore later in the book the importance of trust and confidence for risk-taking in practice.

It must be remembered that what the observee thinks about teaching following the conversation is important if it is to be changed. If the observer can give information that can enable their peer to think differently, that could lead to practice change. For example, Joy was told by her observer during a peer review conversation that 'the group at the back were not engaged in the task; they were talking about something else'. This was useful and encouraged her to think about a range of ways of doing the task differently and monitoring what was happening during group work. Unfortunately, the observer then said, 'You should pick on one of the students and ask them for key points in front of the rest of the class. That should get them to focus'. Using 'you should …' in the context of peer review is inappropriate. If the observee does not believe what is suggested is good practice, then it will not be accepted and the suggestion will also close down opportunities for exploring a range of ideas. The aim is to open up dialogue where both partners can explore ideas for practice. Participants often emphasise the benefits they gain from observing colleagues (Bell and Mladenovic, 2018). Observing in a different context and having the opportunity to see a session from a different perspective can enable the observer to think about their own teaching without being immersed in it. This standing back can enable different things to be noticed and these can be brought to the peer review conversation.

The conversation should not be seen as the end of the process and those involved should think about next steps. This may involve each working on their own teaching, sharing ideas with colleagues or pursuing professional development within a department. Ideas for colleagues to work together on developing practice will be shared later in this book. Peer review insights could be developed into scholarship of teaching and learning (SoTL) where reflection and action to develop teaching becomes more critical, scholarly and public. For many, however, peer review may be the only opportunity they find to explore their thinking about teaching with a colleague, which is why it is vital that this conversation is undertaken in a way that contributes to professional learning. Both parties should come away from the activity feeling enthused about teaching, motivated to continue to learn professionally and with specific ideas about what they would like to do to change an aspect of practice, however small. The conversations about teaching during peer review need to be the best they can be for the staff involved in order to develop practice across the institution.

Critical questions for practice

» Whatever the system of peer review in your institution, can you improve the conversations you have?

» Do you enter peer review conversation, whether observer or observee, with an open mind to learn?

» Is the system flexible enough to deliver real benefits, or is it inhibited by administrative issues?

» Do you see peer review as quality assurance or as professional learning?

Summary

• Paired discussion with a colleague about teaching is an invaluable opportunity.

• Developing a shared sense of expectation before the session improves the chances of a fruitful review.

• An observer may notice different things in a session from the observee – and the difference can be a source of learning.

• If paperwork leads an observer to be judgemental, it's better to set it aside initially.

• Questioning, reflection and critique must underpin review for colleagues to get the most out of it.

• Open questions which avoid assumptions and judgements enhance dialogue.

Useful texts

Sachs, J and Parsell, M (eds) (2014) *Peer Review of Learning and Teaching in Higher Education: International Perspectives.* London: Springer.

The text above provides a summary of peer review of teaching approaches including theories underpinning it and some examples of practice from Western international contexts.

Seek out one-to-one dialogue

If peer review is for many tutors the only regularly scheduled time when they are expected to discuss their teaching, we would argue that further opportunities need to be nurtured in the busy academic schedule. There are of course formal occasions when teaching is on the agenda such as validation and review of programmes, in discussions about modules or perhaps in response to student feedback or data, and in between these occasions there are more informal and serendipitous openings in kitchens, offices and corridors. The challenge is equipping ourselves to make the most of the moments there are, recognising that crowded agendas frequently seem to leave little room for the inquiry and reflection for which we argue at the close of the previous chapter. We turn our attention now to one-to-one conversations and consider how to:

» prepare ourselves to make the most of the opportunities;

» make time for conversations about teaching;

» challenge our assumptions;

» identify new ideas for practice.

Why talk about teaching?

All academic staff have served what Lortie (1975) called 'an apprenticeship of observation', experiencing teaching over many years without being privy to the thinking behind it. Talking with a colleague can help bring to the surface the beliefs we have acquired during this apprenticeship. How we approach conversation will depend on what we unconsciously understand teaching to be and how we anticipate our professional learning as teachers will happen. As we seek to support the next generation of learners in our field, we need to build both knowledge of our discipline or profession and also the ways in which it can be shown to students at different levels. This 'pedagogic content knowledge' (Shulman, 2004) is required, along with knowledge of our particular students, if we are to be able to adjust our examples, materials and methods to meet their needs.

Professional knowledge in teaching involves both understanding theoretical approaches and also developing practical judgement about what to do in specific situations. Theories and research findings about teaching inform our planning and we need practical judgement in the moment to make and re-make sessions. Such judgement about what is best to do in any given situation can develop from experience if it is reflected upon and critiqued in the light of different perspectives. Conversations with colleagues can be an important trigger to help us explore and challenge our teaching in this way.

Professional learning in teaching must be ongoing; situations change, disciplinary and professional knowledge evolves and expectations of students also alter. This requires a personal, ongoing investment in thinking about teaching which can be hard to sustain alone. Conversation with a colleague about ideas and issues is invaluable.

What are we going to talk about?

What we want to talk about may be related to a current agenda in our institution or discipline or a personal priority related to our own teaching. This focus may come from something we think went badly in a session or from a concern that students' work is suggesting lack of understanding in a particular area. We may be alerted to an issue as a result of feedback from students or colleagues. A focus might also come from something that went really well, as we seek to identify what enabled it to be effective. Thinking about teaching tends to be triggered by a concern because we are looking for improvement but building on perceived successes can be equally effective. Impetus to change may also emerge more from reflection on our values than from specific success or challenge: we may question whether our approach aligns with our ideology. We might be looking to change our ways of doing things, even though satisfaction has been expressed by students and colleagues. We may wish to go beyond developing methods to achieve pre-determined ends and seek to question the assumptions which underpin what we do. Engaging in this sort of reflective work has the potential to free us from feeling that we may be stuck in a performative treadmill.

Exploring our lens on the topic

If we are going to have a useful conversation we first need to identify our own perspectives about the chosen topic. This should involve noting and moving beyond those immediate reactions which have triggered our focus in the first place. We develop our thinking, as Mason (2002) says, by *marking* the topic when it occurs and even documenting it.

The first thing to note may well be an emotional response: for example, are we delighted or angry when students challenge our decisions? Our response will be shaped by our own experiences and how these have led to assumptions about good teaching and learning. Our perspective may also be moulded by teaching and learning theories with which we agree and our underpinning values. This outlook is necessarily limited, set in our own personal, professional and cultural context. Engaging in conversation with a colleague will enable another view to be brought to bear, potentially offering a different understanding. Of course those whom we most readily engage in conversation may actually have similar views to our own and without shared inquiry might simply reinforce rather than extend our understanding. In the next chapter we will think about ways to meet colleagues with more diverse outlooks.

Whatever our focus for dialogue, it is useful to call to mind as many occasions as we can where it was a relevant factor. These may be in our own teaching or when we saw others teaching. We might usefully also go back to our own student experience if something similar happened. Careful examination of multiple accounts within our knowledge is a good basis for beginning to spot patterns, ask questions, notice differences.

Getting at our underpinning beliefs however can be tricky as they may well be unexplored. One way to begin unpacking thinking which we have found useful is to envisage an ideal teaching scenario. This might be captured by writing a few sentences describing this scenario on a small piece of paper or by drawing a simple sketch (Figure 3.1). This paper can then be placed on a larger piece where the questions 'What are the learners doing?' and 'What is the teacher doing?' are then answered with a brief summary. This in turn is placed on a third sheet of paper where the questions 'What is the learner's role?' and 'What is the teacher's role?' are answered. Such gradual pulling back from the detail of the session can enable us to tease out tacit knowledge, understanding and beliefs.

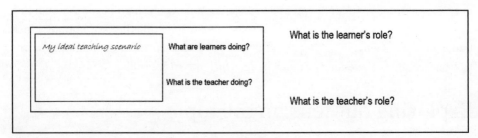

Figure 3.1 Unpacking assumptions about teaching.

The more we can articulate our perspective on a topic then the easier it will be to acknowledge and to step beyond it in the conversations we have. We would argue that taking a critical approach to our teaching requires us actively to gather ways of looking at it beyond our personal standpoint.

Exploring other perspectives

Students, the other half of the teacher–learner dynamic, are experts on their own experience and identifying their views on our area of focus is an important part of the picture. We turn to their perspectives more fully in Chapter 5. Current practice is to collect feedback systematically from groups of students in relation to their experience at the end of each module, and sometimes also mid-module. While formal surveys can be useful, they should not be allowed to inhibit members of teaching teams from establishing a dialogue with students which could inform specific aspects of practice. More questionnaires are unlikely to be welcomed by students or institutional managers, but views can easily be canvassed in a variety of less formal ways. The ubiquity of smart phones and online response platforms enables rapid and simple opinion collection and paper-based approaches are perfectly serviceable. Russell (2007) documents how he regularly sought to try to understand the students' perspective on their learning and his teaching by giving each person an index card or small piece of paper and asking such questions as '*What is the main idea you are taking from today's class?*' and '*What further questions do you have about something we did or discussed?*' (Russell, 2007, p 184). He then developed his next session in the light of these responses. Tailored questions can help prompt reflection of specific aspects of teaching among students. Responses, which are best collected anonymously, are then reflected upon and can be discussed together at the next session, in this way building a shared understanding about learning and teaching.

Tutors who are themselves studying, for example, on a postgraduate diploma in teaching in higher education, can also use this experience to glean insight into some aspects of being a student.

Brookfield (1995, 2017), who has spent years thinking and writing about his teaching in higher education, suggested more than 20 years ago that it is useful to view teaching through the four lenses of self, students, colleagues and literature. Unfortunately, it has been our experience that the extensive research on all aspects of teaching can sometimes be rather neglected, often due to workload and significant disciplinary reading requirements. However, whatever we seek to explore, it is likely that someone, somewhere has thought and written about it in a journal article, conference paper or blog. Not to search for this means missing out on the learning of colleagues wrestling with similar challenges in different contexts and losing the benefit of different ways of seeing, investigating and developing our thinking on practice.

Increasingly, institutions are expecting new lecturers to undertake formal development as educators and it is to be hoped that this is gradually establishing a scholarly and reflective approach as the norm across HE teaching.

Planning for dialogue

Assuming you have decided to talk with a colleague to enable you to understand your own thinking better and to gain a fresh perspective, it is worth now focusing on how to prepare for the sort of constructive dialogue which will help you both. We draw on coaching practices where one person works to help another decide how to move forward, identifying key strategies of listening, explaining, being open and responding.

Critical issues

Conversational strategy

Listening involves listening to understand, not listening to intervene. It is easy to half listen and to think about what one wants to say oneself. Supportive listening requires paying attention to the speaker and to what is being said. This is difficult and requires practice.

Explaining – when talking about teaching the speaker needs to be able to paint a picture of the context and use a description of events which may include anecdotes or stories of experience. Stories are a form of narrative by which social knowledge is shared. They are useful in this context as they connect the world of action with the world of thought (Bruner, 1986). By foregrounding certain aspects of the story we show what we think is significant. When we are explaining it helps if we think carefully about the words we use and not rely on jargon. Phrases such as 'student engagement', which could be differently understood, can distract from unpicking the issues.

Being open requires both people in the conversation trying to avoid being judgemental and looking at the issue from only one perspective. The listener needs to try to decentre from their own viewpoint. It is important that each works hard to understand how their conversational partner is thinking about the issue. This can be done through analytical approaches, such as identifying what contributes to framing problems in this context, including disciplinary perspectives. An empathetic approach is also useful in which the listener tries to stand in the other person's shoes and understand their ways of seeing the topic. Both parties in the conversation need to be prepared to recognise and acknowledge other views and to change their own.

Responding – the purpose of responding to the explanation of the issue presented is for the listener to help their conversational partner to think. Useful responses can be waiting to give the speaker more time, reflecting back some of what has been said and asking questions for clarification such as 'Can you say a bit more about why you think that?' Challenging questions can be used to help generate new ways of thinking about the issue, such as 'What assumptions could you be making here?' And 'What would someone who takes the opposite view say about this?'

This approach can only be effective in a context of trust, mutual respect and an ethical agreement regarding confidentiality. Colleagues who have worked with us to develop paired conversations have found that they can change their thinking about aspects of teaching and consequently effect changes in practice.

Developing critical friendship

Developing conversations to challenge our assumptions and open up new ways of working requires a willing partner, someone we trust who also has an ability to probe thinking and practice: in short, a critical friend. Friendship is crucial if we are to approach any critique of practice without becoming defensive and more entrenched in our own views, unwilling to shift perspective or consider something different. We need to have both challenge and support if our encounters are to lead to development in practice.

Our natural propensity to engage with those who share our views is, in this respect, a danger. One international study of a small group of lecturers suggested that '*interactions with people we perceive to be dissimilar from us are infrequent. Furthermore, perceiving value in those interactions is rare*' (Poole et al, 2019, p 67). At their best critical friendships do involve some shared underpinning values but this is alongside a difference in views about how these can be realised in practice. Of course, it is possible to find such friends within our subject area if colleagues involved actively seek out other sources of learning about teaching, including educational literature.

Formal educational study for lecturers also presents a relatively rare opportunity for academics to talk about teaching with peers from other disciplines. In such programmes staff may be encouraged for the first time to consider the complexity of teaching, they might encounter their first assessed observation and have their first conversations with academics committed to teaching development. Programmes can encourage the practice of inquiry into teaching and the development of critical friendships by espousing reflective practice and offering learning and assessment opportunities which foster conversations with peers about teaching. In our experience, among the things participants most often endorsed as valuable and yielding lasting impact include:

» teaching a short 'micro session' to groups of peers with an experienced facilitator to prompt questions and dialogue about decisions and assumptions;

» planning, delivering and reflecting upon a teaching session with a group of colleagues;

» identifying and researching an aspect of personal practice and explaining this to peers for critical discussion;

» observing disciplinary colleagues teaching followed by shared conversation;

» undertaking an interdisciplinary group inquiry into some aspect of practice and devising a shared presentation, report or poster;

» participation in an 'ideas exchange' when ideas for innovations are swapped with peers.

Project to introduce critical friendship pairs

If critical friendship does not emerge within a teacher's routine, active planning will be required, not least because of the packed nature of academic life to which we have already referred. For this reason we trialled a project encouraging colleagues across an institution to organise one-to-one conversations over a period of about six months. We ran three workshops, initial, mid-project and final to support them. These sessions introduced colleagues to each other, dealt with ethical matters, practised listening and responding skills and offered support from facilitators. We encouraged participants to read Kline (1999) on the role of listening. Feedback from 20 participants who actively engaged in the project was positive. Generally it was considered useful. Some participants reported solving problems in their teaching and for one or two learning was significant: 'for me it was fantastic', 'it is good to try to be in the moment in order to think', 'great to have a conversation with a colleague who has experience and insight', 'people are planning to carry on meeting for the next semester'. Simple logistics derailed engagement for some including timetable incompatibility and the challenge of working across campuses. This is interesting as these are perpetual features of contemporary academic life with which any claim for attention must compete. That institutions have an obligation to take action if they want staff to talk about teaching seems to be indicated by the comments of one participant: '*it felt almost like an indulgence to have a critical friend to talk to*'. Another suggested that 'a scheme like this gives you permission [to have paired conversations about teaching]'. This was a short-term project with a small grant support and it is impossible to know the ultimate impact on thinking and teaching though the evidence is promising.

As facilitators we learnt that:

» it is helpful to practise listening and responding skills before working in this way;

» a structured process can encourage people to engage in this type of conversation;

» the process needs to be facilitated and to be part of an ongoing professional learning offer;

» the presence of a scheme like this, whether many people participate or not, can help support a culture of giving time to conversations about teaching.

Co-planning and co-teaching

Conversations with a critical friend which focus on a particular dilemma or aspect of practice may lead to joint planning and even co-teaching. The best probing dialogue will involve us articulating subject knowledge, values and ethics, views about purposes and processes of learning, and enable often innovative strategies to be shared. Colleagues outside the discipline can raise questions about things we have taken for granted or not noticed about our way of teaching and they may also connect us to wider research in the field. Additionally, if colleagues within a discipline are working together it is likely that the stronger connections they make will improve the way they contextualise the learning of students across a programme, which is often a real hurdle within modular learning.

Planning teaching with a colleague can involve an experienced university teacher working with someone newer to the profession, or new to a particular course or approach to teaching, in a way that enhances the learning of both participants. 'Educative mentoring' (Mackintosh, 2019; Trevethan and Sandretto, 2017) involves the more experienced partner bringing their experience and knowledge to the context but positioning themselves as a co-learner. It is not about one person learning to reproduce what their colleague does in practice; rather, it is about both parties inquiring together into how to support student learning. The process involves articulating the thinking underpinning planning, developing teaching ideas together and focusing on student learning in a particular setting while also drawing out implications for future practice.

This can be followed by co-teaching (Bacharach and Heck, 2007) where both colleagues are involved in teaching the session, which can have advantages for both staff and students. Staff can take different roles in the teaching, including presenting opposing views, identifying the disciplinary thinking being evidenced in a lecture or supporting students in small group work.

Students participating in co-taught sessions generally report greater engagement and learning while staff are more confident, prepared to take risks, adapt their teaching in response to ongoing noticing and feedback and develop a wider range of strategies as well as finding the teaching experience more enjoyable. While the cost of team teaching is an issue, the benefits for students, particularly when they are in large groups, can be significant and for staff it can lead to more reflection on practice, more effective teaching and increased motivation (Bacharach and Heck, 2007). Reflection following the session can increase understanding of issues and strategies and lead to ongoing professional learning and improved practice.

While the critical friendships and co-teaching experiences reported in the literature are usually successful examples, it can be that one or both of the participants do not use listening and conversational approaches to enable the challenging of assumptions, and to prompt research and change. In this case if colleagues are working where there is a system for engaging with different partners, such as the project discussed above, or where teaching groups outlined in the next chapter exist, then finding a different colleague should be readily achievable.

Once established, effective critical partnerships can develop in many ways including those which involve small-scale research projects, often emerging from action research which uses cycles of changing and evaluating practice in order to improve it (McNiff, 2010). A research approach known as 'Self-Study', which involves inquiring into and developing one's own practice with support and challenge from critical friends, is used particularly in North America, Australia and New Zealand and increasingly in some areas of Europe including the UK (Lunenberg, forthcoming; Russell and Loughran, 2007). In addition 'Lesson Study', a group approach to developing practice discussed in Chapter 4, can also be developed as research thus contributing to knowledge and practice in the field (Lewis et al, 2009). This development of an inquiry into practice approach into research activities can be helpful in supporting the research and publication agenda of universities and in building links between research and teaching.

Critical questions for practice

» Why do you organise and undertake your teaching in the way you do? Could you articulate your own underpinning beliefs about teaching?

» Do you believe your students have valuable insights into teaching and learning? When did you last invite them to share their perspective with you?

» Do teachers in your institution think that systematic exploration and discussion of their teaching is a luxury? If so, what could you do to dismantle this idea?

» Where is the time for colleagues to discuss teaching in your workload models/ Continuing Professional Development offering/appraisal process?

Summary

- It is helpful for tutors to explore personal assumptions and views of teaching but it is not easy to do this alone.

- Conversation with colleagues is a vital tool for professional learning which should be built into schedules and encouraged as core practice.

- We can and should prepare ourselves to make the most of opportunities for conversation about teaching.

- Dialogue involves listening, inquiry, exploration of multiple perspectives and an openness of mind.

Useful texts

Bacharach, N and Heck, T (2007) Co-Teaching in Higher Education. *Journal of College Teaching and Learning*, 4(10): 19–26.

This text explores approaches to co-teaching in higher education, including the impact on staff and students.

Brookfield, S (2017) *Becoming a Critically Reflective Teacher* (2nd ed). San Francisco: Jossey-Bass.

In the text above, an experienced higher education teacher shares his learning and process of learning about teaching over the course of his career.

Chapter 4 | Creating and sustaining group conversations

Finding time to meet in groups

If we are looking for opportunities to have the sort of one-to-one conversations discussed in the previous chapter they are comparatively easy to organise, as long as our institution accepts their importance. The logistics of sitting down for dialogue with groups of colleagues is altogether more challenging, as anyone knows well who has tried to find shared space in more than a couple of calendars. However, a great deal of work in universities is undertaken in meetings, such as committees, working groups, project and planning teams. We look in this chapter at how we can include open, reflective conversations of the type we have been discussing in these existing settings and then take action to create new ones.

What's so special about conversations in a group?

The development of collaborative spaces looms large in the design of contemporary university learning environments. There seems to be a widespread acceptance that interaction between students is a valuable, indeed necessary, feature of education for the current age. It is interesting to ponder whether this change in undergraduate and postgraduate provision should not be more fully reflected in staff locations. Creating both the opportunity for, and expectation of, a cooperative approach to our professional learning has advantages for the individual, for teams, for teaching practice and for the institution itself. Principles noted in our chapters on paired dialogue thread through this and if anything are magnified:

» learning from diversity;

» challenging assumptions;

» creating new ideas for teaching;

» generating energy to change practice.

Greater numbers in the conversation mean more support for individuals wanting to try new teaching approaches, take risks, think differently about their practice and potentially transform the way they work. A certain momentum often, in our experience, also enables these groups to share their ideas both with colleagues and leaders.

How do we learn professionally?

Underpinning our argument here is the notion that professional learning best happens 'on the job' with collective examination of ongoing experience. Lave and Wenger (1991) explored the notion that learning in organisations is situated and that knowledge develops through participation in shared activities. This led to their recognition of 'communities of practice', which involve colleagues meeting to share and deepen their knowledge as they work to problem solve or explore issues (Wenger et al, 2002).

In higher education Cox et al (2012) developed a structure for Faculty Learning Communities, in which academic colleagues from across an institution connect for a year focusing on one aspect related to teaching and the curriculum. They think and reflect together and create new ideas for practice. Hadar and Brody (2017) worked in a similar way with teacher educators seeking to build thinking skills in their students. This group lasted for seven years and also identified insights into the way it worked, on which we draw below. Mentoring communities, developed by Felten and colleagues (2013), attended more directly from the outset to the professional learning of members, considering how each learned from the others. They aimed to make their conversations 'transformative' for individuals and for this change to gradually influence the wider institution. Practitioner inquiry groups, which are used at all levels of the education sector, also focus on the importance of tutors developing themselves and their practice and doing this through undertaking practice-based research in a group (Cochran-Smith and Lytle, 2009).

Communities of practice may not work well. They can be hijacked to fulfil a 'performativity' agenda. This is when professionals work strategically to fulfil an agenda based on targets and '*set aside personal beliefs and commitments and live an existence of calculation*' (Ball, 2013, p 215). Rather than leading to initiative and agency, a group working for this purpose can result in conformity and compliance. It can lead to a focus on outputs and less attention being paid to the process and the importance of creating a context for professional learning and teaching. Within a group some colleagues can use power to control the interaction and determine the process. This can lead to a form of 'groupthink' (Janis, 1991) unless the group leader guides the process of listening and challenge.

Challenges to creating conversation groups

The practical difficulties of organising groups for conversations about teaching have already been hinted at: clashing timetables; large or split campuses; availability of suitable spaces when rooms are often at a premium; crowded institutional agendas; finding time simply to do the organising. There may also be constraints in institutional processes and culture which make it difficult to establish these groups, for example:

» institutions specify how staff spend allocated work hours so that anything outside these is seen as extra work;

» professional learning may not be identified as a priority beyond achievement of a minimum level of perceived competence;

» teaching is seen as common sense which does not need thinking about in any depth beyond institutional procedures;

» teaching is seen as a purely individual activity;

» there's an expectation that groups will be organised by managers and will focus on outputs and quick results;

» there's an assumption that having conversations without a clear agenda and plan of action is a waste of time or even subversive;

» there's a perception that the sheer volume of work makes it very difficult for staff to give time to anything outside what is essential for the job, and that collaborative learning is not essential.

It is important, therefore, if we are going to create conversational groups, that we are able to articulate their value so that colleagues including managers can decide whether it is worth committing time and energy to them. The rest of this chapter looks at some ways of creating these groups, how to identify and demonstrate their value and beyond that how to sustain the learning and the learning process.

Creating a conversational culture: more than one kind of group

If purposeful talk about teaching is to become embedded in institutional culture then it must be visible to all. Regular open opportunities to meet must be part of the everyday business of an institution. Examples of these may be familiar: gathering to discuss a paper, hear a short talk from someone about an aspect of their practice or to think together about a shared area of interest. While these are often organised within one department, wider invitations encourage valuable diversity. It is useful to schedule sessions at different times and days of the week so that as many people as possible can engage. These groups should be a normal and valued part of staff learning and alongside them, often emerging from them, other more closed conversational spaces for the development of practice need to be encouraged.

Closed groups and open groups

The mutual respect and trust which underpins the successful critical friendships we looked at in the previous chapter is also essential when working with bigger numbers. It is for this reason that more settled groups are needed alongside open forums. These may well develop if a few people meeting at unrestricted sessions identify that they want to make a greater investment in their professional development by meeting with others. There is of course a risk that those outside such an established group see it as exclusive or cliquey. It's worth emphasising that anyone interested can become a member, it is not about role, experience or expertise, but that once it is formed it needs to be limited to members if it is to work. This is why it is essential that open meetings continue for all and that models of more fixed conversational inquiry groups are explained and encouraged (Figure 4.1).

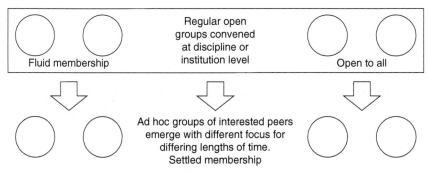

Figure 4.1 Open and closed groups.

Example 4.1

Creating closed groups to inquire into teaching

Monthly lunchtime discussions of about 90 minutes were advertised to all staff. We circulated for discussion by email a short paper about teaching and colleagues were invited to bring along their lunch to eat while talking. Following about six of these meetings the group membership naturally settled at around 10 members of academic and professional staff from different disciplines and areas of responsibility and we arranged lunchtime meetings along similar lines for these colleagues alone. Activities and actions were not planned in advance but emerged through conversation. We agreed to 'notice our own practice' based on the work of John Mason discussed in Chapter 2. This lasted for over a year and resulted in individual practice change plus the group ran 'noticing' sessions at two internal conferences for some 70 staff to share the approach.

'Going out Projects' (Jarvis and Thomas, 2019) were designed to encourage colleagues to engage in conversations in small groups about a self-chosen aspect of teaching and to do this off-campus. Funding was provided by the Deans in two Schools/Departments for small groups to go off campus and have a picnic. The idea was to find a space in the summer term where there was the possibility of extended talk in a different physical place where new ideas could emerge. Picnics can be relaxed and we emphasised as part of this initiative that there were no expectations that the group would produce an outcome or findings. Participants were overwhelmingly positive about the experience, reporting their engagement and coming up with new ideas: '*Ideas seem to burst out when you're not here [on campus]*'; '*With no pressure to deliver anything, we actually delivered a lot*'; '*We came away feeling energised – rare at the end of term*' (Jarvis and Thomas, 2019, p 187). There was evidence of subsequent practice change including the design and implementation of a new multidisciplinary assessment that students subsequently evaluated positively. This experience suggested that even a short time in a small conversational group can have long-term impact.

Leading the group

The role of the leader is to enable group members to learn and develop their professional practice. Hadar and Brody (2017, p 163) in their seven-year study of one learning community saw this role as crucial for effectiveness and argued that they need to:

» clarify the purpose of the sessions;

» create space where learning is possible;

» model good practice;

» respond to what happens in the group.

Clarifying the purpose

The purpose of the groups is professional learning through a conversational approach. The process of learning is fundamental and any topic focus or outputs are the carriers of the learning, not its purpose. For some people this will not be how they understand learning and teaching development and some will not be prepared for the level of introspection or challenge to their views that the approach demands. If people are used to prescribed agendas and quick decision making, the initial phases of group work may appear frustrating or directionless.

The leader must pay attention to any discomfort, identifying ways to enable everyone to participate, helping each to surface what is important to them in relation to facilitating student learning. Having in mind some open questions can help conversation flow such as 'what is learning?' and 'what are the barriers to/ enablers of student learning?' Individuals can be given cards or sticky notes to encourage reflection before sharing.

Creating the space for learning

Professional learning that requires people to reflect deeply on what they do is a risky endeavour. It requires a safe place in which to have what Felten et al (2013) call 'transformative conversations'. Transformation means being prepared to think and act differently; possibly even to re-think long-held beliefs. A safe place is not a place where challenge can be avoided; rather, it is one that enables challenge. Felten et al (2013, p 32) list safety as a key factor in successful groups along with hospitality, courage, honesty, trust, diversity, humility, accountability and friendship. Clark (2001, p 178) argues for the importance of safety, trust and care, while Wenger et al (2002) focus on trust and the building of relationships resulting in a sense of belonging in the group. Hadar and Brody (2017) stress that if there is to be professional risk, such as showing ignorance about a topic in front of colleagues, sharing problems with personal practice or trying something new in teaching, there needs to be a level of psychological safety.

All participants in these sessions are learners, expected to examine specific episodes of their teaching, trying to tease out how and why they work as they do and to help their peers do the same. Sharing thinking makes it visible and enables the questioning of assumptions from multiple perspectives. Leaders must adopt this outlook them-selves – facilitating engagement, listening and sharing but deflecting demands to 'pro-vide the answers' by establishing patterns of inquiry which open up the potential for growth and change.

Modelling the approach

If group members are to take a questioning approach to their practice, to be vulner-able and open to challenge then leaders must demonstrate this in the way they lead and undertake any activities. When one group decided to 'notice' their own practice, each agreed to write down a sentence or two of something they had observed about their teaching. Joy's contribution was first on the table:

When I meet a class for the first time I notice that I talk first to students who are most like me, ie mature white women.

This led to some challenging discussion about age and race as issues in the classroom and showed how noticing might trigger a change in behaviour. Joy was modelling that even if she was seen as a good teacher there were still issues with her practice, she was still open to challenge, to rethinking matters and taking new actions.

Unless the leader is prepared to be vulnerable, others in the group may not be prepared to share any difficult issues of practice and learning opportunities will be diminished. Once a focus like this has been identified and group perspectives have been discussed, understanding can be deepened by exploring related literature. In this instance, Brookfield's (2017) analysis of his own practice in relation to race was useful in developing thinking and ideas for future activities.

Responding to what happens in the group

The leader may be proactive in the beginning, suggesting activities or sharing their own examples of practice but it is vital that they respond to ideas which emerge from the group, not imposing their own direction or dominating the discussion but enabling *'ripples of local sense-making that drive activity'* (Shaw, 2002, p 21). They will be listening, taking views seriously, asking questions, identifying alternative perspectives, recognising and using an appropriate level of challenge, building on the ideas of group members. Although it may appear that conversation is entirely free-ranging, the leader will draw out the threads, identify relevant connections across the institution and with external agendas, enabling understanding of the bigger picture within which their example sits. Relevant research and texts can be identified to enable engagement with the scholarship of teaching and learning (SoTL). One of our groups was keen to undertake educational research and we used Appreciative Inquiry (Cockell and McArthur-Blaire, 2012) partly because conversation is a key part of the approach to data collection. The structured nature of this method requires a sequence of activities to be undertaken, which is helpful where a flattened power structure is desired. This meant the Appreciative Inquiry process, not the leader, drove the work in the sessions.

Identifying value

Close planning for specific outcomes is likely to stifle the essence of creative, conversational dialogue, so there does need to be an element of trust in the process. Having said that, our experience has always been that these exchanges yield real value in diverse ways.

Fun and renewal

Frequently these groups are great fun, something noted by a colleague who had been unable to continue with our group and missed the camaraderie. Wenger et al (2002, p 16) argue that 'fun' is important as it encourages people to engage and helps with commitment, belonging and being prepared to put work into an activity. Sessions allow participants to focus on their enjoyment of their subject and on enabling students to learn and can give a sense of renewal (Clark, 2001).

Creative, purposeful individual practice

The energy and focus of the groups can lead to the development of individual teaching practice. Having explored various perspectives and talked through the thinking behind them, teachers have more options when facing the same situations and can more clearly articulate their reasons for acting, which is important when persuading students to embark on unfamiliar learning activities. Colleagues also have the chance to try strategies supported by their peers. Colleagues from these groups have worked together to obtain bids for funding for research into teaching.

One participant noticed that she spent the first few minutes of every session setting up the equipment to run her PowerPoint slides; meanwhile, students had settled themselves into seats that they were then reluctant to leave if she wished to organise different groups. They had also often become engaged in mobile phone activities that could prove subsequently distracting. After discussion with colleagues in the group she tried welcoming the students into the classroom and directing them to an activity that she placed on the tables, such as a question, some key words to define, or a request to work in small groups summarising the previous session in three sentences. While they were doing this she could then set up the equipment. Her experience and that of the students was greatly improved from this very small change.

Resources and dissemination

Collective enquiries frequently lead to the creation of tangible outputs as members seek to share their insights beyond the group. For example, the Appreciative Inquiry mentioned above led to the creation of resources which were shared with senior managers, and subsequently presented at a teaching-focused academic conference and in a paper for the related special edition of a journal (Jarvis et al, 2017).

Support for the teaching community

We noted above how the group focused on noticing led workshops at two internal learning and teaching conferences. Collective work on reflection, inquiry and supported change can also give individual colleagues the confidence to influence practice within their disciplines. Having developed a clearer sense of their own identity as an educator, they can support peers and groups within their own Schools and bring a new approach to problem solving in their departmental teams.

Sustaining the learning

Institutional leadership

If these groups are to continue and grow within an institution they need to become embedded in the culture. When we set up the 'Going out Projects' (Jarvis and Thomas, 2019) noted above, they were identified by those who participated and by some of their colleagues as valuable. The projects did not, however, continue beyond that year. Although colleagues may have met informally, the encouragement provided by the naming of a project, minimal funding and therefore 'permission' to engage was not continued. This shows that such elements of institutional support are important. Leaders who wish to encourage this type of learning can help by providing structures within which it may happen. This could include modest funding, celebration of work or the promotion of a range of professional learning opportunities including explicit suggestion of, and support for, conversation groups. Leaders also need to be supportive even if things fail or take unexpected turns. Practice change can take time to be effective, sometimes having to navigate initial student dissatisfaction, particularly if the new approach is very different from what has been experienced before.

Using conversation for everyday business

The routine business of universities has many formal opportunities where teaching is considered, for example, in programme and module review, working groups, project and planning teams. If space is allowed to enable conversational approaches to be used these can open up possibilities for course design, content, teaching and assessment. As noted above, where expectation dictates tight agendas and quick decisions, the leader will need to pay close attention to the process and may need to set ground rules such as listening without interrupting and turn taking.

Avoiding stereotypical ways of working can open more opportunities for conversation, risk and change. This might involve using visual supports such as a set of cards with prompt questions for focus. Practical materials, such as coloured threads or long sheets of paper, could be used to map a programme, highlighting unseen connections and making new possibilities visible. Creative working methods can also make it less likely that the talk is derailed by anyone with a particular agenda as the focus is on creating and learning from the materials and artefacts.

Critical issues

Conversation not a committee

After appointment in a role for leading learning and teaching, Joy called her inaugural meeting without agenda or any formal paperwork. Conversation about the nature of learning followed individual activity where each participant, regardless of role, listed words they associated with learning. These were all later typed into a word cloud, which formed a visual reminder of the group's collaboratively articulated foundation. This approach could be disconcerting for people used to a more formal way of working but in this instance it proved liberating and conducive to thinking outside the potential constraints of institutional committee working.

Planning of taught sessions by groups of staff can be enhanced by a conversational approach. This might be particularly useful where the same sessions are to be taught by different colleagues working with a large cohort of students. All too often one person will plan and share slides with colleagues usually without sharing their thinking. Joint planning can both produce a better student experience and enhance staff learning about teaching. A Lesson Study approach (Stepanek et al, 2007) means sessions are devised, taught, reflected on and re-taught by teams. This way of working originated in Japan and is now used in many countries both in the schools sector and increasingly in HE (Calvo et al, 2019; Wood and Cajkler, 2018). Generally, a teaching team first identifies something that is important to teach on a course and that may have proved difficult for students to learn. They then collect information to inform their planning. This can involve the use of Brookfield's four lenses: What is my experience of this? What is the experience of colleagues who have taught this before? What information do we have about the student experience and what does research tell us? Conversation is then focused on planning the session and how the students are anticipated to learn from the resources and activities that have been designed.

Creating a psychologically safe learning space and being prepared to challenge each other in these planning conversations is part of the Lesson Study process.

The planned session, known as the 'research session', is then taught by one or two staff members while others observe the student learning. The session can also be videoed to watch at a later date. Observers subsequently interview some students individually or in a focus group. While what has been learned by the students is important, how the students learned is the focus, as this will inform ways of teaching. Information on student learning is brought to the next team meeting where all perspectives are examined. The focus is on the learning that occurred in the session and how this happened. It is not about an individual staff member's performance. The session is then redesigned in the light of this information and then taught again by different colleagues with the others observing. This re-teaching may occur the next term, for example, depending on groups and timetabling. Following review, the session can be further refined and can be placed in a disciplinary-focused resource bank from which colleagues can draw ideas when they are planning their own teaching on this topic. Knowledge gained can also be used to plan the next stage of learning.

This approach shifts the focus from teaching to learning, which is essential if higher education is to improve. A Lesson Study approach moves beyond 'the students enjoyed it' or 'they were engaged' to statements such as 'giving the students those three examples of the topic enabled them to identify its key elements'. It enables teaching based on data collected in that context and it draws on the knowledge and expertise of all involved together with engagement with research in the field. This approach provides professional learning in teaching, useful for both new and experienced colleagues. It encourages a collaborative approach to developing ways of inquiring into student learning and using this knowledge to drive practice. It provides learning for staff, an enhanced experience for students and connects with the research-informed teaching agenda of higher education. Examples can be written up and form part of the scholarship of learning and teaching.

The main issue here is staff time, although having a small number of 'research sessions' in each School or department each year should be possible. A facilitator or 'knowledgeable other' (Wood and Cajkler, 2018) is not essential to the process but may be necessary when an institution is new to Lesson Study. Resources might be required to develop facilitators with appropriate knowledge of learning, teaching and relevant research. Ethical issues around student participation would need to be identified and resolved, particularly in relation to the observation of learning, interviews and any video recording of sessions.

A Lesson Study approach can be adapted to suit the context and could become part of an institutional professional learning approach for staff and a way of building ongoing improvement in practice.

Critical questions for practice

» When was the last time you talked with your peers about how learning happens in your lecture and seminar rooms?

» Is there an aspect of your teaching you would like to explore systematically with your colleagues? Will you make time to do this?

» Could you adopt a conversational approach in an unexpected situation to unlock a new way of approaching things?

» Are you in an institutional role that would enable you to clearly signal the value of staff groups specifically to talk about teaching?

Summary

- Professional learning happens most effectively in collaboration with colleagues exploring ongoing experiences.

- Closed and open conversation groups need to become an embedded part of institutional cultures.

- Leading effective conversation groups demands responsiveness not control.

- Groups can deliver fun, transformed practice, resources and nourishment for the wider teaching community.

- Conversational approaches can usefully be built into our everyday business.

Useful texts

Cerbin, W and Kopp, B (2006) Lesson Study as a Model for Building Pedagogical Knowledge and Improving Teaching. *International Journal of Teaching and Learning in Higher Education*, 18(3): 250–7.
This article explores the use of Lesson Study to build knowledge and expertise in teaching.

Hadar, L and Brody, D (2017) *Teacher Educators' Professional Learning in Communities.* Abingdon: Routledge.

This is an in-depth study over seven years of one initiative to work in a learning community. This is very useful for people looking for detailed information on the process and issues and provides excellent links to relevant literature.

Wenger, E, McDermott, R and Snyder, W (2002) *Cultivating Communities of Practice.* Boston, MA: Harvard Business School.

The first three chapters of the following are particularly useful and explain the authors' views and experiences of communities of practice and what they consider important for setting up and developing these to add value to the organisation.

An essential perspective on teaching

We now look more closely at a perspective woven through earlier chapters of the book both implicitly and explicitly: that of our students. Brookfield (2017) considers theirs an essential lens through which to grasp a rounded view of academic practice and we have suggested we should pay attention to this in every situation from peer review to Lesson Study. The purpose of doing this is to appreciate better how and where learning happens so that we may design future occasions when it will do so again. If we talk together about teaching and learning, how the one is planned to support the other, then both staff and student experience should be enriched and mutual understanding extended.

Student–staff collaborations in higher education

Student–staff collaboration is increasingly part of institutional processes with universities frequently seeking student perspective on initiatives and expecting their involvement in review and creation of educational programmes. There has also been a rise in students producing learning resources often in discussion with staff. Such materials draw on student understanding of their peers' needs and sometimes provide things staff identify they '*did not have the time available*' to do themselves (Woolmer et al, 2016, p 21). Through creating these resources students may also develop their personal understanding of learning and ways to improve this. Where conversation is at the heart of these interactions they appear to be particularly beneficial.

Example 5.1

Dialogue days

'Dialogue days' were set up in one institution to gain ideas for educational enhancement and to develop student engagement by improving motivation for learning (Ashgar, 2014). Students reported that talking in groups with staff gave a chance for more open discussion than was often the case when representatives attended panels related to modules or programmes. They understood more about the thinking underpinning aspects of practice and were able to give their views. Findings suggested that these days improved staff and students' understanding of each other and in some cases developed better relationships. A suggestion was that this approach could build students' sense of belonging, which can lead to greater engagement in learning.

In some instances staff and students work together to create a module, often as the sessions unfold. Huxham et al (2015) give an account of the co-development of a final-year undergraduate module which aimed to change ways of teaching in order to engage students, give them experiences of authentic approaches to learning in the discipline and enable them to be more self-directive. Bovill (2017) identifies a growing interest in the co-creation of learning and teaching and notes that it is not easy but can be transformative for students and staff. See Bovill's text in this series, *Co-Creating Learning and Teaching: Towards Relational Pedagogy in Higher Education*.

Focus of student–staff conversation

The focus of dialogue will sometimes be helping staff learn and sometimes assisting students though the two overlap and exploring each offers insight on the other.

Staff learning

Strategies to identify students' current understanding to inform staff planning were touched on in Chapter 3. These include 'tickets out of class' (Russell, 2007) where students respond to a question, such as 'what did you find the most useful idea in this session?' Or 'which concept would you like to revise next time?' on a 'ticket' which they leave behind anonymously. This can be done during a session, sometimes following a paired discussion, and could also involve students themselves raising a question which can be written on a card and passed to the end of the row so that the speaker is not embarrassed to ask what they might fear are stupid questions. Polling technology can be used to gather similar information. These approaches can enable staff to focus their teaching more effectively and they may also help students' reflection on their learning.

Another initiative focused on staff learning is the employment of students as academic advisors or pedagogical partners, an approach developed by Cook-Sather (2008). In this model a member of staff is paired with a student who observes a range of classes he or she is teaching and then gives feedback from their own perspective and after discussion with students in the classes. This can enable staff to gain insights into student perspectives and additionally students undertaking this role report coming to understand learning more deeply (Brost et al, 2018).

Student learning

Ways to enable cohorts to think about their learning may be adopted near the beginning of a course or module to encourage students to take ownership of this. Raising awareness of the process of learning, as well as the content of a course, can enable staff and students to develop and articulate a shared understanding of why particular activities are being undertaken and encourage both groups to plan for the 'how' as well as the 'what' of study.

Example 5.2

Picturing the processes

A number of students in a School of Creative Arts reported that they were unclear about how they were expected to learn (Jarvis and Thomas, 2019). Some processes, particularly those developed through experience, are not shared easily with students (Eraut, 2000). Where experts and learners work side by side practices can be seen, copied and realised by learners. In higher education, currently students do not work closely enough to see staff engaged in their primary disciplines, for example, conducting laboratory research, developing products, preparing accounts, so such tacit learning is out of reach.

In order then to surface hidden ways of learning we brought together about 60 colleagues to talk about how people learn in their discipline. Ideas were developed through questioning from those outside their field. They summarised their ideas in verbs and phrases describing learning processes, such as 'experimenting' and 'breaking boundaries'. These words were illustrated in a composite picture as a metaphor for learning in that School. This image then became a focus for staff–student dialogue. Each word/phrase was illustrated separately on a card and packs of these cards were used in activities with students. These activities enabled staff and students to talk about learning in order to develop greater understanding of each other's perspectives in order to inform both teaching and learning. The use of cards to represent learning processes developed to involve a wider range of disciplinary areas and are now used across this university and others to encourage conversations about learning (Figure 5.1).

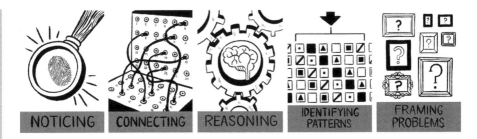

Figure 5.1 Samples of learning processes cards, illustrated by Joel Cooper.

Ways to build the dialogue

Inquiry-based learning

Inquiry-based learning (IBL) may be used to encourage talk about the processes of learning. IBL involves students finding answers to questions posed either by themselves or by staff, through discipline-appropriate approaches. It enables students to talk with each other and with staff about ways of knowing and how knowledge is created as well as learning skills and subject content. This sort of approach has been seen as resistance to the passive learning of a consumer orientation to education with students instead becoming producers of knowledge (Neary and Winn, 2009).

Ovens et al (2011) developed IBL modules involving individual and group-based inquiries on an undergraduate education studies programme. This involved students talking about and investigating ways of learning and led to improved ability to use the inquiry processes necessary to undertake final-year dissertations. There was significant resistance by many of the students to this form of learning as it was seen as more challenging than more traditional forms of teaching used on the other modules on the programme. Working together on a weekly basis enabled the staff to support each other to take the risk to continue with the approach, which the students ultimately appreciated. As it became embedded students who had experienced the change were also asked to come in and talk to new cohorts.

Partnership

Baxter Magolda (Baxter Magolda and King, 2004) has been working with students for many years using what she calls a Learning Partnerships Model, which encompasses a type of joint inquiry. This involves the creation of situations in which students and staff can talk together and share responsibility for developing inquiry. The work acknowledges the challenge of issues around power, which need to be carefully managed or they can derail and limit what is achieved. The different knowledge and skills of all participants are identified and integrated in the collaboration as far as possible. Her approach uses the term 'partnership' which, though (or perhaps because) it is used widely in higher education is both controversial and contested.

Much of the work in which students and staff engage in extended conversations about teaching and learning is similarly framed across the sector as partnership. In a systematic review of literature in the field, Mercer-Mapstone et al (2017, p 1) argue that this approach *'re-envisions students and staff as active collaborators in learning and teaching'.* The emphasis is on working together, the process and its value for participants. This chimes with our focus on conversations involving listening, trust and respect, where space is made for ideas to be explored. This is difficult to do where participants have very different levels of power and where roles and relationships are constrained. Partnership has been construed in many ways (Healey et al, 2014). It can be seen as transformative for both staff and students yet is also critiqued as being used by university managers as part of a performative agenda. Here we focus on the way we have worked to develop conversations about teaching between staff and students in a context we labelled as 'partnership'. The strengths and challenges of the approach are identified.

Student–staff groups

Beginnings

Ten years ago we started to bring small groups of students and staff together to have conversations about teaching. We had two key purposes: to become more effective learners and teachers by exploring each other's perspectives and to encourage others to engage in similar conversation. Framing such a process-focused project in a way intelligible to a sector constructed around outcomes is a tricky task. Some connection to accepted norms must be made to secure buy-in and so our initial focus aligned with an identified institutional priority though later groups would develop their own interests.

We noted in Chapter 4 on staff groups that adopting an inquiry method can help reduce inherent power imbalances which are even more of an issue in student–staff settings and so the project proceeded through a joint inquiry into an aspect of practice. Such inquiry can of course lead to outputs, which will help satisfy expectations and demonstrate the tangible value of the work both for participants and potential future recruits.

There is a tension between outputs and process which can never be wholly resolved. Huxham et al (2015, p 533), when talking about their student–staff working, use mountain climbing as an analogy: '*Mountaineering is an exemplary case of process masquerading as outcome; there are myriad easier ways to the top, hence the purpose is not the peak but the route there.*' So although we did produce publications and resources, which we note below were useful for enhancing the specific aspects of practice under collaborative scrutiny and indeed for making a case for our continuation, these were just a positive by-product. Our purpose was in fact the conversation, the group itself and learning how to do it and how to learn through it.

Organisation

The first job in organising sustained student–staff conversation to take place over a semester or an academic year is to engage a number of staff and students. In our project, staff involved already had accepted responsibility for developing learning and teaching as they were members of a designated departmental group. Later, other colleagues who expressed an interest in what we were doing volunteered to be involved. Students were recruited through advertisements and payment for two hours' work a week was offered. Practically, we were able to meet only for a two-hour, session fortnightly, with the other two hours being used for data collection, reading and supporting activities. Two students and one member of staff per School were involved initially as we aimed to lessen the possibility of students being reluctant to speak if they were in a minority. A research fellow was also part of each of the projects, partly to research the process and partly so that she could be consulted by staff and students about appropriate ways of collecting and analysing data. This was important so that staff were not seen by students as being the experts in undertaking inquiries and also because most colleagues involved were not familiar with education research methods.

The first project we undertook was organised over one semester and involved one student–staff group and one topic of focus. Over time we tried different group formulations: having one topic of focus but a number of different small student–staff groups exploring this in different settings or having a number of different topics but bringing all participants together regularly to share challenges and ideas. As we expanded we always aimed to have some of the students or staff in each group with experience of being in a previous group so that there was continuity in understanding the process.

Process

Creating a context where both students and staff can listen and talk with each other, share differing perspectives and offer and accept challenge is difficult. We drew on the idea of a learning community, discussed in Chapter 4, and on ways of creating conversations explored in Chapters 2 and 3. While building a context for conversation with students and staff is similar to that for staff-only groups, the importance of talking about and modelling the process is heightened. Assumptions need to be shared and explored. Issues of trust, confidentiality, duty of care and boundaries are highlighted due to differences in the power held by students and staff in an educational context. While building relationships within the project can lead to open conversations it can be difficult for both groups once they are back in the classroom and in a different relationship. While leaders have a duty of care for all participants this is accentuated where students are involved.

More specific work on building relationships and communication was undertaken in student–staff groups, including a range of activities to identify what we had in common and how our differences could be used effectively. We later documented some of these activities in a 'Partnership Learning Communities' resource for the UK Higher Education Academy (Jarvis et al, 2016).

Modelling ways of listening and responding that offer support and challenge was perhaps our most important tool for developing conversations. As leaders we had to be particularly aware of student initiatives in conversation which could be missed and lead to lack of confidence in contributing. Two examples of why this is important follow.

Example 5.3

The wall: a compelling metaphor

In one of our group conversations, one of the students mentioned that there seemed to be a 'wall' between students and staff. There followed a wide-ranging discussion about what this might look like, how it was built, what it influenced and what would happen if it could be taken down. The group decided to employ an illustrator to depict five stages: building the wall, looking through the wall, connecting through the wall, taking down the wall and working without the wall. This metaphor was then used across the university to discuss barriers and ways of breaking them down. Boxes of large plastic bricks were used for activities with different groups to explore this issue, and these are available as a loan educational resource. These bricks were also used by a member of staff and two students when they talked with the staff at the Higher Education Academy about the impact of their conversations. A small conversation led to a big impact!

This example highlights a key difference in the leadership role depending on whether the focus is on the process or only on the outcome. Our intention was to pay attention to the process and to give it time. In our experience being prepared to be slow at the beginning of a project and not rush to try to achieve specified outcomes means that conversations can lead to new ideas and initiatives. In dialogue the route and end point are not pre-determined and this is what leads to the creation of new knowledge. We are not involved in meetings but in conversation.

Example 5.4

Good student – good learner

A student–staff group were working on materials for new students. The conversation was about what makes a 'good student'. Some people were using the terms 'good student' and 'good learner' interchangeably whereas a student argued that she saw them as very different things. This was then explored through conversation and it became clear that a good learner could be seen as someone who explored their discipline widely, took risks in learning, and was enthusiastic and keen to share their learning, whereas a good student was compliant in reading what was expected, following assessment guidelines, working out what the course leader wanted and working to produce this. What challenged the staff was the students thought that the university pushed the students towards being the good student and not the good learner. One staff member was considerably challenged by a student who noted that the staff were obsessed with assessment and that was often the first thing they talked about and returned to repeatedly in sessions, whereas the member of staff had always perceived that it was the students who were assessment orientated. This led to a re-think for this member of staff and others in the group about how they talked about assessment. Insights from this conversation were then presented at staff seminars, to new staff and to senior managers.

Value

If participants are to engage in groups, and if institutional managers are to support them, then they must recognise their value. For some people this will be about individual growth and change, while connecting with institutional plans and external agendas will also be important. We worked to research the value to students (Dickerson et al, 2016) and identified employability and research skills that students had gained through the process. In addition, many reported a greater understanding of learning and confidence in contexts with staff. One student went on to become a student-representative co-ordinator in her School, while another was subsequently employed by the university as a student engagement officer and later a lecturer. He now engages his own students in conversations about teaching and learning. Two brief excerpts below from participants identify the value of the process for them.

Example 5.5

Personal accounts of partnership impact

From a student

'The biggest impact had to be the ability to separate emotions from my work. I was influenced by the staff I worked with to not take things personally. I previously believed that any work I produced was a personal reflection on myself. I got to see what my work looked like from the perspective of a teacher. As a result, I believe I am able to be more constructively critical of my work… Realising that we were part of the same community also allowed me to be more open and contributive.'

From a staff member

'Working in this way with students unlocked something important in my head: why plan with staff alone about how to battle problems students face? Talking honestly with learners who were actually experiencing my teaching and much more in touch with the challenge made complete sense. Together we could shed light on ways through, rather than me making (inaccurate) assumptions about what was happening. It led to a new way of being a teacher for me: much more listening than talking; not a performance but a shared endeavour. The result of this was more inclusive and empowering for the students in my sessions.'

(Accounts from personal communications with authors)

It is worth noting that while the transformation of student experience in these projects was great, it was limited to a relatively small number of individuals. However, a shift in staff perspective will affect the learning and experience of all the cohorts they teach.

To demonstrate value to those outside the group we made our work visible. The energy and impetus to effect change generated by the conversations resulted in the production of resources for students on aspects of education such as using feedback or making the most of your first year at university, and for staff on approaches to develop students' disciplinary reading and writing skills. A video for students on using assignment feedback was produced.

As leaders we made sure we were connected to external events so that groups presented at external conferences and networks and we set up exchange visits with a group at another university working in the same way. As noted above, our aim was not to produce outputs but they arose through the conversations and the resulting commitment to 'do something' to develop practice. The growing visibility of the work enabled it to be recognised within the institution and to be developed by others. Some staff members from the original groups set up their own conversation opportunities with students.

Sustainability

The tension between process and output looms large when it comes to sustaining this sort of work – simply because group process is difficult to see. While outputs can be useful to show the value of the group in a context where tangible materials, resources and papers are seen as markers of success, this can lead to others to mistake this as the purpose of the group. When trying to extend the conversation process across our institution it was hard for us to show people who had not been involved in what we had been doing. What was visible was what had been produced, such as a new teaching strategy or resource, while the process was invisible. One colleague, for example, explained that they already worked with students as partners by 'getting them to do things' for the module. This was not a conversational approach and would not be a perception of partnership we would wish to encourage. We therefore aimed to set up a network of people who identified themselves as being involved in some form of staff–student work that they labelled as 'partnership'. This could enable us all to explore the process together and to all develop our understanding of the process. We came to realise as we worked across the institution that while for us the conversation was the starting point, and a focus and outputs emerged from this, other staff and students were focusing on developing materials, and from this work conversations developed.

Sustaining and building our work beyond the local proved to be an issue. We set about this using a variety of methods – collecting and publishing case studies, informal lunches and drop-in sessions, poster conferences, small online surveys of network members, an email newsletter and by encouraging and celebrating the work and success of individuals both at internal and external conferences. For us being able to associate the network with an institutional narrative of partnership also helped. Connecting to a recognised agenda and strategy enables participation from a wider range of colleagues.

An expectation of partnership in institutional processes around teaching does create opportunities for a conversational approach to be adopted, for example, in programme committees, reviews and working groups. It is important to continually consider the mutuality and trust we have been outlining if student involvement is not to become tokenistic. Involving students in projects at an early stage, where they are expected to influence activities and outcomes, is important, as is recruitment, training, payment and clarity of expectation. In this way we have seen conversation with students used to help tackle tough challenges around assessment and inclusion.

Critical questions for practice

» In a complex and evolving age how important is it that your students develop ways of learning for themselves in the discipline?

» To what extent do you explore with your students the process of learning in your discipline? Do you make assumptions about what they want/need without asking?

» Are you encouraging your students to be good learners or good students?

» Will you seek out the opportunity to engage students so you can learn about your teaching and their learning together?

Summary

- Students and staff need to engage in open conversation if developed understanding of learning is to be achieved.

- Power, responsibility and conventional interactions must be addressed if conversations are to transform learning.

- Inquiry and partnership are useful ways to collaborate effectively. These must be underpinned by mutual respect and openness to learn – from both staff and students.

- There is value and substance in the conversations themselves – not just in the things they produce.

Useful texts

Huxham, M, Hunter, M, McIntyre, A, Shilland, R and McArthur, J (2015) Student and Teacher Co-Navigation of a Course: Following the *Natural Lines* of Academic Enquiry. *Teaching in Higher Education*, 20(5): 530–41.

This article describes a group of staff and students creating an inquiry approach to disciplinary learning.

Jarvis, J, Dickerson, C, Clark, K, Stockwell, L and Clark, A (2016) Partnership Learning Communities: A Resource Produced for the Higher Education Academy. [online] Available at: www.advance-he.ac.uk/knowledge-hub/partnership-learning-communities (accessed 10 February 2020).

We created the resource above to share ideas of questions to consider and activities to undertake when initially setting up a student–staff conversation group, although it could also be helpful for new staff groups as well.

Magolda, M B and King, P (eds) (2004) *Learning Partnerships: Theory and Models of Practice to Educate for Self-Authorship.* Sterling, VA: Stylus.

The text above gives powerful examples of student–staff working together and the impact on participants.

Chapter 6 | Building reflective conversation in assessment of teaching

Prepare for a positive exchange

Conversations around the assessment of a member of staff's teaching may not at first thought seem to offer the sort of opportunity for open and honest talk for which we have been arguing, but our experience is that these too can be mutually beneficial exchanges. The ways these conversations are undertaken will shape how staff perceive teaching and its development, either as a one-off assessment of competence or the beginnings of ongoing professional learning.

The setting requires additional preparation because of the way dialogue is set in the context of assessment but this is an area of university business where high-quality engagement about the challenge of teaching is both possible and desirable.

The assessor will be conscious of the inherent power imbalance and should take steps to address this if the dialogue is to be effective. Trust, mutual respect and positive regard are still needed as the basis of interaction whether the discussion follows a teaching observation as part of probation, a formal course of study or is about achieving the recognition of a professional award.

It is useful, as we noted in Chapter 2, to be aware that the conversation may be understood differently by those in it and without noticing this it is easy to be frustrated or to talk at cross-purposes. Here are some things that might help both the assessor and the assessed to consider.

» Is the observee anxious? Tension is understandably very commonly mentioned in staff reflections around teaching observation and it is difficult to focus on developing your practice if you are fretting about whether you passed.

» Is teaching seen, by the assessor, the person being assessed and by the institution, as a personal performance rather than a complex activity where the context must also be carefully examined? How teaching is viewed will shape the content and direction of the conversation.

» Is the assessment viewed by either party as 'hurdle-jumping' divorced from learning? This can happen if assessment in general is seen solely as a test of current competence rather than a practice which supports and involves learning.

» Is the observee there by choice? Mandatory completion of a course or requirement to obtain professional recognition can be an obstacle if it is understood as performative activity designed principally to meet a management agenda. It is of course possible to meet someone else's agenda and still achieve something of value.

The assessor is the one with whom responsibility for an effective conversational assessment begins. If they want talk which has the potential to drive positive thinking about practice and action planning for change, then they need to model a way of being as a teacher that involves inquiry and critical reflection with the aim of encouraging this approach. How they might do that is the focus of this chapter.

Promoting inquiry and critical reflection

The assessor should work hard to maintain Senge's (1990) balance between inquiry and advocacy. They need to seek to understand the other's perspective and to contribute from their own experience. They need to choose words and frame the discussion as a chance to learn. Acknowledging that the person being assessed is a disciplinary expert with academic autonomy and responsibility for building their subject teaching knowledge focuses the attention on what they bring to the session and on the importance of proactivity for professional learning. Clearly, evaluation in any of the situations we mention will have to meet some given criteria. However, UK Professional Standards Framework (UKPSF) descriptors and typical teaching observation learning outcomes tend to seek practice which is 'effective', 'appropriate' or 'successful', which indicates little about the specific manner in which this might be achieved. If the experience and independence of a colleague is to be validated, it is important for an assessor to be in touch with their own assumptions and be prepared in dialogue to challenge or expand these if necessary. If authenticity is a key aspect of teaching success then it follows that one type of practice will not suit all – even within the same disciplinary settings. This may sound obvious but as we noted when we discussed peer review it is easy to make assumptions and to judge another's practice in relation to our own.

Critical issues

Ask, don't tell

A new computer science lecturer completed a teaching observation successfully but their observer took the position of expert judge and said

→

they 'should have asked students by name to contribute'. This apparent instruction dominated the observee's recollection of the conversation to the exclusion of other aspects. The feeling that their behaviour, which had purposefully evolved over a number of weeks interacting with shy class participants, had not been fully appreciated overrode other reactions. As opportunities for extended conversation with experienced peers are so seldom on our timetable this seems to be a rather wasted exchange, which might have been redirected simply by asking 'Could you have asked...?' The difference between a statement and a question, between 'should' and 'could', fundamentally influenced the opportunity for this to be an effective learning conversation.

Conversations around assessed teaching observations

Documentation around observations can be drafted to encourage assessors not to lose sight of a wider sense of teaching in their discussions. If the focus is on 'performance' factors alone this will tend to narrow the scope of any subsequent conversation. Overemphasis on pace, clarity, content, technique, etc may inadvertently encourage observees to restrict their reflection. If, however, paperwork also prompts thought about such matters as the context, aspects of inclusion, checking of learning, underpinning evidence, even learner autonomy and teacher identity, this can open up conversation. Framing the observation with a critically reflective dialogue embodies a view of teaching as complex and contextual and encourages attention to be paid to the many factors at play in any given session.

Often these observations are critical points at the beginning of an academic career as they must be passed to complete probation. An observer should try to stay aware of unexplored assumptions about teaching as performance, which can make lack of success a particularly painful experience for the observee. On the plus side, a supportive discussion, even after a difficult session, can be a real affirmation and boost to confidence. Being failed following observation of a challenging lecture or workshop could be counterproductive, undermining the nurturing of skills, which is usually the goal of the whole exercise. It's possible for a conversation deconstructing the session to establish the observee's reflective approach to practice and their awareness of the challenges they face such that the observer does not feel failure is appropriate. Furthermore, it is useful if room is left for a second observation without any recording of failure. Ideally these second chances open the door to constructive discussion, adaptation, possibly shared planning, and demonstrate an approach to teaching which is not isolated nor performance orientated and models it as a learning, evolving activity. It is important to note that conversations should not shun challenge; indeed, this is a key part of moving thinking on.

Critical issues

Respectful challenge

Karen recalls seeing a highly organised seminar full of great activities and meticulously planned interactions which nevertheless left two young men whispering to each other 'What's going on?', 'What do we have to do?'. When Karen discussed this with the lecturer it became clear that they considered that these students were not capable of following what was to be done in the class. The conversation shifted to the expansion of higher education and whether these students 'should even be here'. At this point it was necessary to challenge these views and offer different perspectives, in a way that acknowledged potential difficulties for staff in planning appropriate activities and where support for this could be obtained. As there may be few opportunities for colleagues to be challenged about their assumptions about education, it is important that this is done in this context and that it happens in a way that does not lead to defensiveness but to change.

It is helpful if the observer enquires about and takes account of the local teaching culture in their conversation as this will inevitably shape the notion of how teaching ought to be conducted in the disciplinary context being observed. There might, for example, be very didactic instructions for new lecturers, or mentors might have encouraged 'learning by observation' and what a new lecturer notices may not be entirely helpful. For example, they might accord undue importance to a personal attribute, as where one colleague decided 'I must learn to tell jokes if I am to be a good lecturer like X'. It is not uncommon in large teaching teams for one staff member to prepare slides and for everyone to be told to use them so that students 'have the same experience'. There are contradictions inherent in this, not least the idea that different staff with different students using the same materials give everyone the same experience. In addition, if the user has not had enough time to familiarise themselves with materials it can be impossible to use them intelligibly.

Critical issues

Delivery at any cost?

Karen recalls watching one staff member speaking to very professional-looking slides for about 20 minutes and being unable to follow the narrative at all, when suddenly the argument became clear and engaging. In the subsequent conversation the lecturer explained that the change happened at the point where they completed 'delivery' of compulsory slides provided to the whole team and began to use their own. An assessor in this situation should always be alert to the bigger picture, the context and constraints faced by the observee. If appropriate they might seek in wider conversations with the department to challenge practice which puts tutors in this position in the first place, though that clearly goes beyond the observation itself.

A model for effective practice in assessment conversations

Graham et al (2012) describe a 3-D model (Discover, Deepen, Do) for developing newly qualified teachers as professional learners, which can be used to support effective assessment conversations. The first D, Discover, involves identifying significant aspects of practice that can form the focus of discussion. The second, Deepen, requires strategies to gain a fuller shared understanding of this area of practice, while the third, Do, focuses on taking the learning forward into new practice.

Before beginning a conversation, Graham (2013) suggests that the observer reflects on situations where they have had their own teaching sessions observed, including those times when that has not gone as well as one might have hoped. It is important to remember that teaching is an emotional experience and that learning to teach can be a *'complex, bewildering and sometimes painful task'* (Maynard and Furlong, 1995, p 10). Graham argues that empathy and building rapport are essential if learning is to occur. Mezirow (1990, p 13) notes: *'By far the most significant learning experiences in adulthood involve critical self-reflection'*. If this is to occur, as we noted in earlier chapters, the right environment has to be created.

Discover

The first part of the post-observation conversation requires the observer to listen to the teacher talking about what they noticed and what they thought about what happened in the session. It is necessary to start with the teacher's own concerns as this is where they will put their future energy. The observer can use paraphrasing and reflecting back what has been said, as well as questions such as 'why do you think that?' Often the person being observed only talks about negative aspects of the session and the observer needs to balance this by pointing out what went well. The observer can help to lower the power differentials in the relationship by recalling aspects of their own practice that have caused them concern. Not everything in a session can be discussed and both participants need to identify the areas they are going to focus on. If there is something that the observer thinks is important that the teacher has not noticed then the observer can use focus questions, for example, 'What did you notice about the timing of the session?' to help the teacher identify aspects of practice that they need to think about. It is important that the teacher who is being observed identifies that the areas of focus are important as this will provide the motivation for further development.

Deepen

Deepening understanding of the chosen areas of focus involves questioning assumptions, thinking from different perspectives, drawing on prior experiences and from research and writing in the field. If the observation is part of a programme of study the observee may have been asked to identify one or two resources, such as journal articles, which informed their planning. They may, however, be unaware that teaching and learning is a topic of research, or that there are journals on the topic in their field. Either way it is useful during the conversation to give examples of research evidence and identify relevant sources of further information.

It is important that the observer models a questioning approach, asks open questions and seeks evidence for statements such as: 'You say that they were not interested, how do you know that?' or 'What did students do or say that indicated that they had understood that point?' This models how teachers take a critical approach to practice. This deepening is a shared endeavour and it's important that the observer does not suggest that the teacher should have done something specific. Actions will always depend on a range of factors, including some contextual knowledge which the observer will lack. As Usher et al (1997, p 130) note, *'The question which always faces the practitioner – how ought I to act? – does not have an invariant answer.'* This does not mean that the observer cannot talk about their own experience, as it is important to share experiences in a professional learning conversation, but this should be seen as one way of thinking about the topic, not the only way.

This part of the conversation aims to support both participants in their thinking about teaching. If this way of working together on one occasion can be seen as a temporary mentor–mentee relationship, then both parties can learn. Hudson (2013, p 771) identified that mentoring new teachers led to *'reflecting and deconstructing teaching practices for mentors' own pedagogical advancements'*. If the observer shares what they have learned through the conversation, this helps lower power differentials inherent in the context and identifies that professional learning in teaching is ongoing. In the final stage of the process the participants need to draw together the threads of their conversation and decide what they are going to do to develop practice.

Do

Here both participants identify what they have learned and implications for practice. The teacher who is being assessed needs to say what they will do to develop an aspect of practice. It needs to be something possible and not too ambitious or it is unlikely to happen in the busy and often stressful context of developing a new role. Discussion needs to take place about how the change will be evaluated and what will be seen as success. The assessor can also suggest ideas for support including offering to be observed themselves, ideas for reading, or learning and teaching development events. What will be written about the session needs to be discussed, particularly if there are specific criteria that need to be addressed on a feedback form. This needs to be seen by the teacher who has been observed before it is submitted as a formal document. The observer needs to be clear if there are concerns about passing the observation and what is available within their institution to support future success.

Example 6.1

3-D model in practice: observation of a seminar

Joy observed a seminar led by a new young male lecturer. Eight students were present. Three young male students sat together on one side of the room, two more mature male students sat individually on the other side and three young female students sat in a row at the back.

After the session the lecturer reported that the session had not gone as well as he had hoped. While he had been able to engage the three young male students in animated conversations on the topics involved, the two other male students had produced one question each when asked 'Have you any questions?' but when he said to the female students 'You ladies haven't said anything, have you anything you want to say?' they remained silent.

In the 'Discover' part of the conversation Joy pointed out all the positive features of the session: his own enthusiasm and knowledge of the subject; his examples of application of the concepts he was explaining, which were both from personal experience and from a range of international sources; and the clear evidence of understanding shown by the three participants who were involved in discussion with him. His use of summary slides to identify key points was a clear strength as was his use of a list of terms with definitions. He needed to retain all these aspects, so it was important that he was aware of them and could use them in future. They decided to focus on the issue of oral participation of students.

They *deepened* understanding by talking about questions such as 'Do you have to talk in class to learn?' 'What do we know about quiet learners from literature such as Akinbode's (2016) article on the quiet learner and the quiet teacher?' 'What does the furniture arrangement have to do with interaction in the room?' 'How and why might you ask students to work in groups?' Joy also shared her own experience (noted in Chapter 4) of identifying that she talked first with students most like her when she met a new group. The lecturer noted that he found students most like him, young and male, the easiest to engage with. This sharing of perceptions identified this as an issue of practice that could be explored, not a personal failing. It also became clear that inquiry into personal practice is important. A key question explored was 'Why do you want students to say anything in a session?' The lecturer decided that for him the most important thing was that this would enable him to know what they had understood, or not, so he could adjust his session accordingly. Ways to gauge learning were then discussed, including activities in pairs and small groups and ways of asking and answering questions that did not require speaking to the whole room.

Towards the end of the conversation the lecturer decided that what he would *do* in the next session would be to ask the students to form self-chosen pairs or groups of three and to undertake a task together in which they matched key terms with given definitions and then work out an example of each. As they worked on these he would go to each group talking about what they were doing and identifying good examples. He would then choose a good example from each group, which he would read out. Later he would identify a good example from each group but would ask group members to read them out so that they could hear their voice in the room and gain confidence in speaking in these situations.

Example 6.2

3-D model in practice: observation of a supervision

This observed session was of a one-to-one dissertation supervision of a masters student by an experienced research academic who had supervised students at this level in international contexts. Consent to this observation had been gained from the student in advance. The lecturer presented the observer with a detailed plan of what would be covered in the 50 minutes allowed. The session proceeded with the lecturer giving clear explanations and examples of where the student needed to deepen aspects of his work, and explained what he needed to do next. She then summarised the session. After the session she said that she felt that it went well, the student was a good student and would achieve a good outcome.

Joy agreed that the student had been given very clear directions and explanations and had seemed to understand what he was expected to do it and the next steps he had to undertake. Joy noted that she had been amazed at how much had been covered in the session and that she had initially thought that the plan was over-ambitious but she had been mistaken and that all aspects had been undertaken. As there was no clear lead from the lecturer about what she felt she needed to develop, Joy decided to explain her own reactions to this successful session.

Joy explained that she had been surprised by the way the supervision had been undertaken because she herself undertook these sessions at a slower pace, followed the lead of the student initially and she expected them to do a lot of the talking. She said that having watched this session she now thought that perhaps she should increase her own pace and give more explanations of approaches and perhaps a higher level of direction. She said that she thought there was a continuum of level of control with Joy at the lower end and the lecturer at the higher end. As they both had successful outcomes it was not a question of one being better but of difference.

A conversation followed about different approaches to teaching and learning, what it meant to be a masters student, particularly in relation to initiative and decision making, the implications of the short time frame for completing a dissertation and disciplinary differences. Joy had been unsure how much initiative the student was taking in relation to his dissertation and during this discussion the lecturer explained that the student had sent her questions in advance, as he had not wanted to look too ignorant in front of an observer.

Also the student emailed questions and ideas between sessions, to which she responded promptly, so there was more of a dialogue going on than appeared in the session. It is important that this type of information is surfaced during conversations about observations as the observed session is only a small part of the teaching and learning that is taking place.

At the end of the session both Joy and the lecturer agreed that they had learned a lot. The lecturer noted that she had never discussed her supervision practice with anyone and that it had been useful to reflect, particularly on assumptions about roles and responsibilities within supervision and on what 'teaching' meant in this context. She decided that she would do two new things that she hadn't thought of before and that had arisen in the conversation. First, rather than telling the student at the end of the session the next steps he should take, she would ask him and then agree these together. Second, rather than summarising the session herself she would ask the student to send a brief bullet point summary so she could see what was taken away from the session.

In these two examples there were different routes to a change in practice. The first came from a focus identified immediately by the person being assessed. In the second new insights came through the conversation itself.

Conversations around teaching competency

Some conversations about teaching will occur where questions about a lecturer's competency have been raised. In many contexts today this is likely to be due to student feedback, although it could also be reports from staff to managers, or managers' observations. When working with a colleague in this context, getting the best conversational relationship is vital. As Scott (2002, p 108) writes in her text *Fierce Conversations* one of the key mistakes in one-to-one sessions is the assessor '*doing most of the talking*'. It is vital to listen and give time to understand the colleague's views and perspectives, to allow emotions about the issue to be surfaced and to acknowledge the impact on the person's well-being. How the colleague understands teaching and what constitutes 'good' teaching needs to be understood as it is difficult to work towards a practice one disagrees with. Far better to start with what the colleague sees as their strength and working to make this stronger. Using questions and examples around particular aspects of practice can enable the colleague to start to find their own solutions to issues.

Example 6.3

Using conversation where competence is an issue

A lecturer had repeated feedback from students that his lectures were 'boring', that they were long and difficult to understand. Many stopped attending his lectures. Colleagues offered suggestions for interactive lectures involving a range of activities he considered childish. An initial conversation with an academic developer aimed at identifying what he saw as important in his practice. This was that students needed to know certain pieces of information and understand particular key concepts. His preferred method was a transmission model. The conversation then developed into co-planning a session together where ways of thinking about teaching could be surfaced and new ideas for practice developed. It was helpful that the academic developer was from a different discipline, as the need to explain disciplinary knowledge and assumptions to an 'outsider' could help the lecturer to be explicit to students. The next lecture involved: fewer slides; fewer words on slides and a break after every 20 minutes where students worked in pairs to answer a question about a concept. The conversations continued with joint planning of a series of lectures, which led to successful changes to practice.

This form of ongoing conversation is expensive in staff time but was effective in this case. Changing the thinking underpinning practice can lead to ongoing small changes. A mandated change that is not fully accepted or understood is unlikely to lead to ongoing development of practice. It is of course worth noting that this approach cannot always work: some people are unable to change or develop their teaching for a range of reasons.

Professional recognition conversations

Conversations around professional recognition as a teacher in higher education can be iterative in that applicants often engage with colleagues over a period of time about what is needed as they prepare their claim. As they need to show how they meet identified criteria, participants may seek help around interpretation and to find out 'what the assessors want'. The candidate may work with a more experienced colleague in a mentoring relationship to assist professional learning through conversation and the construction of narratives (Clarke et al, 2002). Narratives of practice can be explored for underpinning values and assumptions and for ways of working that relate to designated criteria.

The whole process can be performative and of limited value in terms of practice development, but equally it can enable colleagues to think critically about their teaching, sometimes for the first time. Applying for recognition can enable '*individuals to articulate who they are and what it is they do, interactively with a knowledgeable other*' (Ashgar and Pilkington, 2018, p 142). Colleagues may initially be unaware of literature around teaching so identifying what is relevant to read is a useful part of these pre-assessment conversations. Sometimes colleagues find it difficult to move away from an unexamined view of teaching and aim to 'tick the boxes', though for others the process may help them to understand what they do and therefore have more control over the choices they make in the future.

An assessment conversation at its best helps the candidate articulate values, purposes and examples of practice. Setting up this environment to enable all involved to learn requires attention to the conversational process described earlier in this book. As Ashgar and Pilkingon (2018) note in their research on professional dialogue in professional accreditation, trust between people is essential. However, it is likely that there will be a sense of performing the conversation for a particular purpose, which can inhibit learning. Additionally, there are issues around confidentiality that may inhibit the candidate from being frank. As a starting point this process should enable a candidate to articulate their practice, while at its best it can initiate and support ongoing development as a teacher.

Critical questions for practice

» How do you approach assessment conversations, whether assessor or assessed: are you aware of your own assumptions, open to learn, ready to listen?

» What is your focus in an observed teaching session: student learning or performance of the tutor?

» If you have watched a colleague teach do you 'shoot first' with a judgement and ask questions later or do you open with inquiry?

Summary

• Careful thought and mutual respect should be the basis of assessment conversations.

• Unacknowledged assumptions about teaching from observer or observee can undermine these dialogues.

⟶

- When evaluating a colleague's teaching, don't jump to conclusions. Remember teaching is complex and contextual: discover, deepen, do.

- Assessment offers a chance to demonstrate critical reflection and promote inquiry into teaching practice.

- Well-managed assessment dialogue can lead to learning for both participants.

Useful texts

Ashgar, M and Pilkington, R (2018) The Relational Value of Professional Dialogue for Academics Pursuing HEA Fellowship. *International Journal for Academic Development*, 23(2): 135–46.

This article describes a research project to understand the benefits and challenges of using a dialogic approach in an assessment context.

Graham, S (2013) Enhancing Professional Learning Conversations. In White, E and Jarvis, J (eds) *School-Based Teacher Training: A Handbook for Tutors and Mentors* (pp 33–40). London: Sage.

The chapter above illustrates the use of the '3-D' approach with a new teacher.

Talking at the heart of our teaching lives

In this book we have explored ways in which conversational approaches can engage university teaching staff in thinking about, critiquing and developing their teaching. We have identified ways to use critical reflection with others to enable learning about teaching. We argue that teaching is a complex social process enacted in a particular cultural context involving knowledge, skills, values and attitudes. This complexity means ongoing professional learning is necessary for effectiveness and to generate new ideas and approaches. Conversations we have described can enable colleagues to learn from each other and can nurture leadership of teaching.

We have used examples to highlight how dialogue can encourage lecturers to inquire into their practice. Some instances have involved scholarship and research, generating knowledge beyond the local. Many individuals have changed the way they teach; staff and students have reached new insights and understanding of teaching and learning. Unexamined and poor practice has been investigated, and courses have been redesigned creatively and effectively.

We argue that conversational methods can galvanise when used wherever university teaching staff work in groups, for example, reviewing programme design, implementing new quality or assessment approaches, and planning modules and sessions. We have evidence of this sort of impact within our experience but it does not happen without leadership. Leaders are needed to structure the process, to bring knowledge and understanding of teaching, of inquiry, research and scholarship. Conversation may be natural but if it is to be deployed to effect change it must be planned and used purposefully.

By leaders we do not confine ourselves to those with designated roles though they obviously have an important part to play. We believe it is vital that leadership of teaching is nurtured across an institution in disciplinary communities among all staff engaged with teaching. We will suggest the sort of steps needed from educators at all levels of the university, but first we note a number of possible constraints on effective progress.

» Conversations about teaching that challenge assumptions can be personally uncomfortable and can disrupt long-held beliefs about the quality of one's own work and what it means to be a 'good' teacher.

» Conversations that explore assumptions about institutional practices can be uncomfortable for universities if they lead to pressure for change that conflicts with centrally managed versions of teaching.

» Business structures and disciplinary tribalism frequently combine to produce a silo culture. Working across boundaries and collegiately can be difficult.

» A perception of teaching as solely an individual activity which is evaluated as personal performance side-lines the importance of context and undermines the sense of community.

» Increasing use of zero hours contracts can also lessen the sense of community and limit opportunities to work collegially.

These 'bigger-picture' issues will need to be identified when using a conversational approach, partly so that they can be talked about and potentially tackled, but also so that leaders can be realistic about what can be achieved and be prepared to be pro-active over an extended time-frame, celebrating small successes along the way.

Staff leading conversations about teaching

Any member of staff involved in teaching can take a lead in working with colleagues to develop educational practice. As Frost (2018, p 93) identifies, 'non-positional teacher leadership' does not depend on role or appointment. If you are going to take up opportunities to engage others in conversations to change teaching you will want to think first about your own teaching, reflect on why you teach the way you do and identify areas of interest. Once prepared you can seek out opportunities to engage with colleagues. Often challenges or frustrations of practice will surface in casual exchanges in offices, kitchens and corridors, and you can pick these up with a purpose, perhaps following up a conversation by sharing a relevant journal article which addresses the issues raised. Chapters 2 and 3 look at one-to-one dialogue and offer many pointers about how you can start to build critical friendships with colleagues around you. You may also seek to connect with others outside the university, perhaps in an online group focused on an area of interest in teaching, perhaps by attending a conference. You might use social media such as Twitter to find external colleagues with similar areas of professional interest. Reaching beyond your local network will increase your knowledge of what is happening in the sector and alert you to relevant events and scholarship.

You might also wish to create a new group. Charlwood (2014), for example, initiated a conversational group for a small number of HR professionals. Organising an environment with comfortable chairs, tea and cake, she enabled colleagues to discuss their work and arising issues and solutions. This informal setting encouraged people not to 'stand on their roles' and to listen to each other. Most participants reported making changes to their work practices after engaging in these sessions. Charlwood used a particular form of leadership known as Host Leadership (McKergow and Bailey, 2014), which draws on the way we organise social events. It involves inviting colleagues and then creating a space for reflection and sharing of perspectives within a 'listening' culture. The host ensures the conversation flows and connects ideas but does not dominate the group. After the session the leader gathers, documents and shares any ideas that emerged and maintains momentum by arranging the next meeting. This is akin to the approach described in Chapter 4 where we considered conversational staff groups and could be used within a teaching team, across a disciplinary area or more widely advertised within an institution.

If you do not have a role in relation to learning and teaching some colleagues may question why you are creating a group. However, we have found objections usually melt away as colleagues realise they are gaining something from the meetings. It is likely anyway that you have acquired informal authority by virtue of your interest or knowledge about learning and teaching. If you can secure modest funding for refreshments, for example, from a manager or a grant from a learning and teaching fund this can also help your group's status. This might be especially useful if you are working in a highly managed area where some colleagues perceive the 'permission' such support offers as a necessary prerequisite.

Leaders with formal teaching roles taking a conversational approach

Leaders with formal roles are expected to be there when teaching is being talked about and can be proactive in pursuing a conversational approach in everyday settings. If working with an established group, such as a programme or module team, it can be effective to begin by facilitating an open conversation. It is possible to offer both support and challenge, adopting the sort of open and questioning methods discussed throughout the book and highlighting the importance of inquiry and scholarship in underpinning decision-making. This will need persistent attention where this is not the expected way of working, where colleagues have not undertaken exploration of teaching before and where they have not problematised what they are doing. Assumptions about teaching and students can be perpetuated if a leader is not there to challenge and keep focus on student learning and practice building.

Ideas given above and in Chapter 4 should be of use to leaders who wish to create groups with colleagues who are interested in teaching. A topic can be identified and advertised in advance or a meeting can be called with only a broad teaching focus allowing an area of focus to emerge from conversation. Thomas (2016) had a role one day a week for developing teaching in the School of Creative Arts at our university. Like Charlwood (2014) the group she created involved sharing cake to contribute to an informal, relaxed and mutually connected atmosphere. She also used Host Leadership, drawing on ideas of hospitality to engage colleagues in exploration of their teaching approaches and issues of diversity and inclusion.

Those with formal roles may want to hone their skills of conversational leadership perhaps through undertaking a peer coaching course or engaging with writing such as that of de Hann (2005) who outlines different approaches to asking questions and facilitating consultation. Flinn (2018) in his work on professional learning in leadership argues that methods adopted should align to the leadership approach chosen. Those who advocate conversational practice must therefore develop skills such as listening, creating a space for reflection and challenge, sense-making and documenting learning in group settings.

Ideally this work will include colleagues in a range of disciplines so that a network of those interested in collaborating and moving practice forward across an institution is built. Gradually leaders will need to encourage others to assume leadership roles. Supporting others in this way is fundamental if there is to be departmental and institutional impact. Persistence, the ability to work steadily over many years and a long view on practice development is needed to grow this capacity. Our experience is that while this bottom-up approach to the leadership of teaching is vital, cultivating it is a slow process. Being explicit about expectations of leadership may be helpful. Colleagues may need to be encouraged to see that no formal role is needed to do this work and that leadership can be facilitative and not controlling. Such matters, even though we think we are demonstrating them clearly, can be overlooked perhaps because they are not what peers are attuned to notice.

Those whose role enables them to provide support for others in leading groups can help greatly by offering a framework to encourage varied conversations. For example, the paired thinking about teaching initiative in Chapter 3 offered a structure for providing workshops, a forum for connecting and a contact for participants during the programme. Without some level of organisation, initiatives do not become embedded in institutional practice. Activities such as the 'Going out Projects' in Chapter 4 could become a regular feature of professional development with a system for advertising the opportunity, distributing any funding and publicising subsequent practice developments. Such modest organisation from acknowledged leaders also provides 'permission' for staff to participate.

Cherrington et al (2018) describe a pan-university learning community that grew over three years to comprise 248 participants from a staff of approximately 2,100. Small group hubs connected by a steering committee provided a work-based learning opportunity together with practice change across the university. They found that a steering group that took responsibility for logistical and organisational issues enabled the staff to engage in the conversations and development of practice. In addition, support and funding from senior managers was vital. If the aim is to engage as many staff as possible in taking initiative to lead their own professional learning in teaching and to contribute to practice development then leaders need to support conversations around teaching but not to control them. The importance of facilitated staff-led activity needs to be considered when working to build an institutional culture that enables this type of work to flourish.

Institutional leadership

Those in institutional roles will realise that the strength of their university lies in its staff. Gratton and Gosham (2002, p 222) assert that in order to build *curious, questioning and creative organisations*' everyone must be encouraged to engage in purposeful conversations about practice. In a sector focused on learning we might expect this to be relatively straightforward. However, this is not the case. Baxter Magolda and King (2004, p 259) note there are *'constraints that faculty face in accessing opportunities for rich dialogue around their teaching'*. She suggests that these can include the perception that teaching is an individual, technical activity and that there is little support for reflection and collaboration. While it is necessary to identify what the barriers are in our own institutions, we focus on some of the strengths which leaders should aim to foster so that problems may be overcome.

Features of a flourishing learning organisation
An embedded understanding of teaching as complex

Institutional approaches which move beyond a simplistic view of teaching towards an expectation that it will be the focus of ongoing learning, inquiry and scholarship could involve an overall structure for professional learning for staff that includes continuing opportunities for work-based learning. These might include:

» post-induction opportunities for disciplinary-focused learning such as co-teaching and Lesson Study with appropriate workload allocation;

» funding and time allocation for participation in teaching groups and networks;

» thriving writing groups, opportunities for sharing/mentoring expertise in educational research;

» courses offered to develop educational practice;

» promotion opportunities for leading teaching;

» funding for research in teaching and undertaking doctorates in teaching in disciplines.

Established structures that recognise and reward groups working to improve student learning rather than focusing solely on individual performance

Awards could be made at institutional level to recognise teams that have collaborated to develop effective learning approaches for students. Nomination criteria could be used to enable students and colleagues to identify impact on learning. Individuals might be rewarded to the extent that they have enabled peers to succeed and learn. Achievements could be included in teaching and learning routes to promotion.

A focus on long-term practice building rather than short-term 'quick-fixes' that respond to external drivers and inhibit longer-term practice building

Institutional leaders can help staff and students understand the role of external drivers such as satisfaction questionnaires and league tables, acknowledging their importance for the institution and how they are dealt with. Alongside this they will also identify strategies for building lasting practice development into the organisation of teaching. This would include ensuring that teaching duties are allocated with a focus on building expertise in teaching particular disciplinary topics and providing funding for teaching projects which seek impact beyond one course or calendar year.

Distributed leadership of teaching change

Distributed leadership *'characterized by multiple authorities which are constructed in the interactions between people'* (Woods, 2016, p 155) identifies that power and authority to enable change exists at all levels across an institution. Here we argue that for this to be effective, strategies must be put in place to build capacity for staff at all levels to lead and develop practice within their disciplines. This might mean:

» encouraging managers to identify and endorse, but not micromanage, less formal leadership;

» routinely offering support to individual initiatives – for example, by funding refreshments for inquiry teams or conversational groups;

» fostering projects about learning and teaching, and collating and sharing findings;

» commissioning inquiry around identified challenges;

» inviting staff to run groups and linking these to formal decision-making committees;

» coordinating 'learning lunches' where staff from all levels come together to share ideas;

» provision of coaching and courses to build leadership skills at all levels.

Thriving cross-university connections; reduced 'silo working'

In Cherrington et al's (2018) pan-university learning community a key aspect was engaging and empowering leaders to emerge and work with colleagues across the institution. They identified the importance *of 'institutional mechanisms that enable community participation to be acknowledged and supported through time and institutional funding'* (Cherrington et al, 2018, p 308). Another facilitating factor was providing a framework to connect initiatives so work was not fragmented across the institution. This can also help to dismantle any sense that discipline areas are competitors.

Conversations to change teaching

In this book, we have argued the case for the important role of conversations between colleagues in enhancing professional learning in teaching and in improving practice in higher education. Purposeful conversations focused on student learning have the potential to transform teaching in local and institutional contexts. Leadership is key and this involves leadership undertaken by individuals in relation to their own practice and by positional leaders working to build a conversational culture in the institution. Education effects change in lives and societies; that it is why it is important to build change in teaching one conversation at a time.

Critical questions for practice

» What do you do to encourage an understanding of teaching as complex and a focus for inquiry?

» What priority do you give to creating time and space for conversation about teaching?

» Do you encourage leadership of teaching in others?

» Where you are involved in conversation about teaching, how might you ensure this contributes to institutional development?

Summary

• An understanding of teaching as a complex activity, which requires ongoing professional learning, must be embedded at institutional level.

• Conversational approaches to teaching development need to be nurtured. This is a long-term project.

• Leadership of teaching must happen at all levels: individual; disciplinary; and institutional. Leadership does not mean control.

• A focus on conversations to change teaching is essential if we are to be effective educational institutions.

Useful texts

Bolden, R, Jones, S, Davis, H and Gentle, P (2015) *Developing and Sustaining Shared Leadership in Higher Education.* London: Leadership Foundation for Higher Education.

The above text could be helpful to institutional leaders as they explore the use of distributed leadership.

Charlwood, H (2014) Anyone for Tea, Cake and Conversation? *SDF Digest: A Practitioner Journal for HE Staff Development*, 2: 42–8. [online] Available at: http://sdf.ac.uk/cms/wp-content/uploads/2016/07/sdf02-full.pdf (accessed 10 February 2020).

The text above explains a small-scale project to bring together a group of work colleagues for conversations to change practice. It shares the rationale, approach and impact and could be useful for teachers contemplating leading a staff group.

Cherrington, S, Macaskill, A, Salmon, R, Boniface, S. Shep, S and Flutey, J (2018) Developing a Pan-University Professional Learning Community. *International Journal for Academic Development*, 23(4): 298–311.

This text shares the practice of building a cross-institutional learning community and could be useful for leaders of teaching.

References

Akinbode, A (2016) The Quiet Learner and the Quiet Teacher. *LINK*, 2(1). [online] Available at: www.herts. ac.uk/link/volume-1,-issue-2/the-quiet-learner-and-the-quiet-teacher (accessed 13 January 2020).

Ashgar, M (2014) Staff and Student Experiences of Dialogue Days: A Student Engagement Activity. *Innovations in Education and Teaching International*, 53(4): 435–44.

Ashgar, M and Pilkington, R (2018) The Relational Value of Professional Dialogue for Academics Pursuing HEA Fellowship. *International Journal for Academic Development*, 23(2): 135–46.

Bacharach N and Heck, T (2007) Co-Teaching in Higher Education. *Journal of College Teaching and Learning*, 4(10): 19–26.

Ball, S (2013) The Teacher's Soul and the Terrors of Performativity. *Journal of Education Policy*, 18(2): 215–28.

Baxter Magolda, M and King, P (2004) *Learning Partnerships: Theory and Models of Practice to Educate for Self-Authorship.* Sterling, VA: Stylus.

Bell, A and Mladenovic, R (2008) The Benefits of Peer Observation of Teaching for Tutor Development. *Higher Education*, 55: 735–52.

Bohm, D (1996) *On Dialogue.* London: Routledge.

Bovill, C (2017) Breaking Down Student-Staff Barriers: Moving Towards Pedagogic Flexibility. In Kinchin, I and Winstone, N (eds) *Pedagogic Frailty and Resilience in the University* (pp 151–62). Rotterdam: Sense Publishers.

Brookfield, S (1995) *Becoming a Critically Reflective Teacher.* San Francisco: Jossey-Bass.

Brookfield, S (2017) *Becoming a Critically Reflective Teacher* (2nd ed). San Francisco: Jossey-Bass.

Brost, C, Lauture, C, Smith, K and Kersten, S (2018) Reflections on That-Has-Been: Snapshots from the Students-as-Partners Movement. *International Journal for Students as Partners*, 2(1): 130–5.

Bruner, J (1986) *Actual Minds, Possible Worlds.* Cambridge, MA: Harvard University Press.

Calvo, A, Bianco, G and Fueyo, A (2019) The Potential of Lesson Study Project as a Tool for Dealing with Dilemmas in University Teaching. *International Journal for Lesson and Learning Studies*, 7(2): 124–35.

Charlwood, H (2014) Anyone for Tea, Cake and Conversation? *SDF Digest: A Practitioner Journal for HE Staff Development*, 2: 42–8. [online] Available at: http://sdf.ac.uk/cms/wp-content/uploads/2016/07/sdf02-full.pdf (accessed 10 February 2020).

Cherrington, S, Macaskill, A, Salmon, R, Boniface, S, Shep, S and Flutey, J (2018) Developing a Pan-University Professional Learning Community. *International Journal for Academic Development*, 23(4): 298–311.

Clark, C (2001) Good Conversation. In Clark, C (ed) *Talking Shop: Authentic Conversation and Teacher Learning.* New York: Teachers College Press.

Clarke, M, Power, A and Hine, A (2002) *Mentoring Conversations and Narratives from the Tertiary Experience.* Perth, Australia. Paper presented at the Annual Conference of the Higher Education Research and Development Association of Australasia (HERDSA).

Cochran-Smith, M (2004) The Problem of Teacher Education. *Journal of Teacher Education*, 55(4): 295–99.

Cochran-Smith, M and Lytle, S (2009) *Inquiry as Stance: Practitioner Research for the Next Generation.* New York: Columbia University, Teachers College Press.

Cockell, J and McArthur-Blaire, J (2012) *Appreciative Inquiry in Higher Education.* San Francisco: Jossey-Bass.

Cook-Sather, A (2008) What You Get is Looking in a Mirror, Only Better: Inviting Students to Reflect on College Teaching. *Reflective Practice*, 4: 473–83.

Cox, M, Richlin, L and Essington, A (2012) *Faculty Learning Community Planning Guide.* Los Angeles: Alliance Publishers.

de Haan, E (2005) *Learning with Colleagues: An Action Guide for Peer Consultation.* Basingstoke: Palgrave Macmillan.

de Hann, E and Burger, Y (2014) *Coaching with Colleagues: An Action Guide for One-to-One Learning.* London: Palgrave Macmillan.

Dickerson, C, Jarvis, J and Stockwell, L (2016) Staff–Student Collaboration: Student Learning from Working Together to Enhance Educational Practice in Higher Education. *Teaching in Higher Education*, 21(3): 249–65.

Eraut, M (2000) Non-Formal Learning and Tacit Knowledge in Professional Work. *British Journal of Educational Psychology*, 70: 113–36.

Felten, P, Dirksen, H, Bauman, L, Kheriaty, A and Taylor, E (2013) *Transformative Conversations: A Guide to Mentoring Communities Among Colleagues in Higher Education.* San Francisco: Jossey-Bass.

Flinn, K (2018) *Leadership Development: A Complexity Approach.* Abingdon: Routledge.

Flinn, K and Mowles, C (2014) *A Complexity Approach to Leadership Development: Developing Practical Judgement.* London: The Leadership Foundation.

Frost, D (2018) HertsCam: A Teacher-Led Organisation to Support Teacher Leadership. *International Journal of Teacher Leadership*, 9(1): 79–100.

Gosling, D (2014) Collaborative Peer Supported Review of Teaching. In Sachs, J and Parsell, M (eds) *Peer Review of Learning and Teaching in Higher Education: International Perspectives* (pp 13–32). London: Springer.

Graham, S (2013) Enhancing Professional Learning Conversations. In White, E and Jarvis, J (eds) *School-Based Teacher Training: A Handbook for Tutors and Mentors* (pp 33–40). London: Sage.

Graham, S, Lester, N and Dickerson, C (2012) Discover – Deepen – Do: A 3D Pedagogical Approach for Developing Newly Qualified Teachers as Professional Learners. *Australian Journal of Teacher Education*, 37(9): 43–66.

Graham, S and Weston, K (2013) Better Together. *Engage*, Autumn, 5. London: Leadership Foundation. Project report. [online] Available at: https://uhra.herts.ac.uk/bitstream/handle/2299/13822/906822.pdf?sequence=2 (accessed 14 January 2020).

Gratton, L and Ghoshal, S (2002) Improving the Quality of Conversations. *Organisational Dynamics*, 31(3): 209–23.

Hargreaves, A (2008) *The Persistence of Presentism and the Struggle for Lasting Improvement.* London: Institute of Education.

Hadar, L and Brody, D (2017) *Teacher Educators' Professional Learning in Communities.* Abingdon: Routledge.

Haig, N (2006) Everyday Conversation as a Context for Professional Learning and Development. *International Journal for Academic Development*, 10(1): 3–16.

Healey, M, Flint, A and Harrington, K (2014) *Engagement through Partnership: Students as Partners in Learning and Teaching in Higher Education.* York: Higher Education Academy.

Hudson, P (2013) Mentoring as Professional Development: 'Growth for Both' Mentor and Mentee. *Professional Development in Education*, 39(5): 771–83.

Huxham, M, Hunter, M, McIntyre, A, Shilland, R and McArthur, J (2015) Student and Teacher Co-Navigation of a Course: Following the *Natural Lines* of Academic Enquiry. *Teaching in Higher Education*, 20(5): 530–41.

Janis, I (1991) Groupthink. In Griffin, E. (ed) *A First Look at Communication Theory* (pp 235–246). New York: McGraw-Hill.

Jarvis, J (2018) Is Teaching Systemically Frail in Universities and If So What Can We Do About It? *LINK*, 3(2). [online] Available at: www.herts.ac.uk/link/volume-3,-issue-2/is-teaching-systemically-frail-in-universities-and-if-so-what-can-we-do-about-it (accessed 13 January 2020).

Jarvis, J, Dickerson, C, Clark, K, Stockwell, L and Clark, A (2016) Partnership Learning Communities: A Resource Produced for the Higher Education Academy. [online] Available at: www.advance-he.ac.uk/knowledge-hub/partnership-learning-communities (accessed 10 February 2020).

Jarvis, J, Thomas, R, Rosella, T, Smith, J, Nimmo, S, Hodgkinson, J, Glass, L, Clark, K, Barlow, J and Baker, T (2017) 'Find the Gap': Can a Multidisciplinary Group of University Teachers Influence Learning and Teaching Practice? *Practice and Evidence of Scholarship of Teaching and Learning in Higher Education*, 12(3): 446–64.

Jarvis, J and Thomas, R (2019) Reframing Spaces for Staff Learning. In Bilham, T, Hampshire, C, Hartog, M and Doolan, M (eds) *Reframing Space for Learning: Excellence and Innovation in University Teaching* (pp 185–198). London: IOE Press.

Kinchin, I and Winstone, N (eds) (2017) *Pedagogic Frailty and Resilience in the University*. Rotterdam: Sense Publishers.

Kline, N (1999) *Time to Think: Listening to Ignite the Human Mind*. London: Ward Lock.

Klopper, C and Drew, S (eds) (2015) *Teaching for Learning and Learning for Teaching: Peer Review of Teaching in Higher Education*. Rotterdam: Sense Publishing.

Kreber, C (2009) The Modern Research University and its Disciplines: The Interplay between Contextual and Context-Transcendent Influence on Teaching. In Kreber, C (ed) *The University and its Disciplines: Teaching and Learning Within and Beyond Disciplinary Boundaries* (pp 19–31). London: Routledge.

Lave, J and Wenger, E (1991) *Situated learning: Legitimate Peripheral Participation*. New York: Cambridge University Press.

Lewis, C, Perry, R and Friedkin, S (2009) Lesson Study as Action Research. In Noffke, S and Somekh, B (eds) *The Sage Handbook of Educational Action Research* (pp 142–54). London: Sage.

Littleton, K and Mercer, N (2013) *Interthinking: Putting Talk to Work*. London: Routledge.

Lortie, D (1975) *Schoolteacher: A Sociological Study*. Chicago: University of Chicago Press.

Lunenberg, M, MacPhail, A, White, E, Jarvis, J, O'Sullivan, M and Guðjónsdóttir, H (forthcoming) Self-Study Methodology: An Emerging Approach for Practitioner Research in Europe. In Kitchen, J, Berry, A, Guðjónsdóttir, H, Bullock, S, Taylor, M and Crowe, A (eds) *International Handbook of Self-Study of Teaching and Teacher Education* (2nd ed). Singapore: Springer.

Mackintosh, J (2019) Educative Mentoring. *LINK*, 4(1). [online] Available at: www.herts.ac.uk/link/volume-4,-issue-1/educative-mentoring (accessed 13 January 2020).

Mason, J (2002) *Researching Your Own Practice: The Discipline of Noticing*. London: Taylor and Francis.

Maynard, T and Furlong, J (1995) Learning to Teach and Models of Mentoring. In Kelly, T and Mayes, A (eds) *Issues in Mentoring* (pp 10–22). London: Routledge.

McKergow, M and Bailey, H (2014) *Host: Six New Roles of Engagement*. London: Solutions Books.

McNiff, J (2010) *Action Research for Professional Development*. Poole: September Books.

Mercer-Mapstone, L, Dvorakova, S, Matthews, K, Abbot, S, Cheng, B, Felten, P, Knorr, K, Marquis, E, Shammas, R and Swaim, K (2017) A Systematic Literature Review of Students as Partners in Higher Education. *International Journal for Students as Partners*, 1(1). [online] Available at: https://mulpress.mcmaster.ca/ijsap/article/view/3119 (accessed 13 January 2020).

Mezirow, J (1990) How Critical Reflection Triggers Transformative Learning. In Mezirow, J (ed) *Fostering Critical Reflection in Adulthood: A Guide to Transformative and Emancipatory Learning* (pp 1–20). San Francisco: Jossey-Bass.

Neary, M and Winn, J (2009) The Student as Producer: Reinventing the Student Experience in Higher Education. In Bell, L, Stevenson, H and Neary, M (eds) *The Future of Higher Education: Policy, Pedagogy and the Student Experience* (pp 126–38). London: Continuum.

Ovens, P (2011) *Developing Inquiry for Learning: Reflecting Collaborative Ways to Learn How to Learn in Higher Education*. Abingdon: Routledge.

Poole, G, Iqbal, I and Verwoord, R (2019) Small Significant Networks as Birds of a Feather. *International Journal for Academic Development*, 24(1): 61–72.

Quinn, L (2012) *Re-imagining Academic Staff Development: Spaces for Disruption.* Stellenbosch: Sun Press.

Russell, T (2007) How Experience Changed my Values as a Teacher Educator. In Russell, T and Loughran, J (eds) *Enacting a Pedagogy of Teacher Education: Values, Relationships and Practices* (pp 182–91). Abingdon: Routledge.

Russell, T and Loughran, J (eds) (2007) *Enacting a Pedagogy of Teacher Education: Values, Relationships and Practices.* Abingdon: Routledge.

Roxa, T and Martensson, K (2009) Teaching and Learning Regimes from Within: Significant Networks as a Locus for the Social Construction of Teaching and Learning. In Kreber, C (ed) *The University and its Disciplines: Teaching and Learning Within and Beyond Disciplinary Boundaries* (pp 209–18). London: Routledge.

Scott, S (2002) *Fierce Conversations.* London: Piatkus Books.

Senge, P (1990) *The Fifth Dimension: The Art and Practice of the Learning Organisation.* New York: Doubleday.

Shaw, P (2002) *Changing Conversations in Organisations: A Complexity Approach to Change.* Abingdon: Routledge.

Schön, D (1987) *Educating the Reflective Practitioner.* San Francisco: Jossey-Bass.

Shulman, L (2004) *The Wisdom of Practice: Essays in Teaching, Learning and Learning to Teach.* San Francisco: Jossey-Bass.

Stacey, R (2001) *Complex Responsive Processes in Organisations: Learning and Knowledge Creation.* London: Routledge.

Stepanek, J, Appel, G, Leong, M, Mangan, M and Mitchel, M (2007) *Leading Lesson Study: A Practical Guide for Teachers and Facilitators.* London: Corwin Press.

Stevenson, J, Burke, P and Whelan, P (2014) *Pedagogic Stratification and the Shifting Landscape of Higher Education.* York: Higher Education Academy.

Thomas, R (2016) Going Out on a Roll: Cake, Conversation and Critique. *LINK*, 2(2). [online] Available at: www.herts.ac.uk/link/volume-2,-issue-2/going-out-on-a-roll-cake,-conversation-and-critique (accessed 13 January 2020).

Thomson, B (2013) *Non-Directive Coaching: Attitudes, Approaches and Applications*. Northwich: Critical Publishing.

Trevethan, H and Sandretto, S (2017) Repositioning Mentoring as Educative: Examining Missed Opportunities for Professional Learning. *Teaching and Teacher Education*, 68: 127–33.

Usher, R, Bryant, I and Johnston, R (1997) *Adult Education and the Postmodern Challenge: Learning Beyond the Limits.* London: Routledge.

Wenger, E, McDermott, R and Snyder, W (2002) *Cultivating Communities of Practice.* Boston, MA: Harvard Business School.

Wood, P and Cajkler, W (2018) Lesson Study: A Collaborative Approach to Scholarship for Teaching and Learning in Higher Education. *Journal of Further and Higher Education*, 42(3): 313–26.

Woods, P (2016) Authority, Power and Distributed Leadership. *Management in Education*, 30(4): 155–60.

Woolmer, C, Sneddon, P, Curry, G, Hill, B, Fehertavi, S, Longbone, C and Wallace, K (2016) Student Staff Partnership to Create an Interdisciplinary Science Skills Course in a Research-Intensive University. *International Journal for Academic Development*, 21(1): 16–27.

Zeldin, T (1998) *Conversation.* London: The Harvill Press.

Index